NO ONE WILL BE IMMUNE

and other plays and pieces

BY

DAVID MAMET

★

★

DRAMATISTS
PLAY SERVICE
INC.

NO ONE WILL BE IMMUNE AND OTHER PLAYS AND PIECES
1994, David Mamet

TH NO JOY IN IT
© 1991, Antaeus

...ILL BE IMMUNE
Copyright © 1990, David Mamet
as an unpublished dramatic composition

All Rights Reserved

SPECIAL NOTE

TABLE OF CONTENTS

ALMOST DONE

ALMOST DONE

A Monologue

ALMOST DONE is a monologue for a woman. She is talking to her child. The child is not on stage.

But I remember we were walking in the snow, and I was cold. *(Pause.)* I was very cold. He said that we were almost home. That I should think ahead to when we'd be home. We'd be sitting by the fire, it would be warm and I would think back when I had been in the cold, how long ago that seemed. How very long ago. How funny I had been upset that I was cold, when all I had to do was think ahead, and then it would be passed. It was passing all the time. Even the time that I spent thinking of it passed the time I would be home, he said and looking in the fire. I would be warm. And it would give me visions. You remember, he said, visions you have looking in the fire. Of the future most times. Feelings that you have. Yes, I said. Think ahead, he said. I was so cold, I said 'I'm cold.' I know, he said but think ahead. Soon you will be warm, looking back, it all will be as one. Soon. I would think I will be older then, looking in the fire, and soon I will be old. I will be married, I will have a home. Now I am young, I am a child, I am a baby now but then I will be old. I will look back on thinking this. And I would smile, I smiled then in the cold; I will think how simple a child is, worrying about things which are passing. And soon I will have my own. And this will be lost, sometimes, I will think back to it, perhaps I won't think of it for years, and one day, for a story to tell, to quiet him or to amuse him I will tell him of when I was young. I thought ahead and smiled, I will tell him how *cold* I was. Or I will think ahead to when I'll have him and smile at the story I will tell him. Someday he will tell it

7

to his children. You remember when you were so cold. Well I will tell you something that my mother told me. Once when she was young, as you are young, she was out walking with her father, my grandfather, in the cold. And she was very very cold, and when he tells it he will think of me, I thought. Kind thoughts, as if something had just been made clear to him which was not clear before. Something that he knew, but did not know he knew. I thought of him, what it would be to have a child, I was so young myself. Walking home, almost home, he said, I knew we were far from home, we were not almost home at all, but it was passing, while I thought of it, and he was happy, he was content, perhaps he saw something different from what I saw. Or his notion of time was different. I thought: One day I will get up and wake up my husband, I will say we must go to the hospital, I'd thought of this day for a long time. Dreaming at the fire, I thought, when I will have a child. He will get up, and get dressed, silently, I thought: One day you will be grown and this is what I'll tell you: One night I woke up during the darkest part of night and told your father: I am going to have the child, and we went to the hospital. We'd wanted you a long, long time. A long, long time, and you were coming to us. That night he was frightened for me, I think. I knew he was, we went, he held my hand. I'd waited for that such a long, long time. Once I was a child, I thought of you, now I think of my parents, walking in the cold that day, he said just think ahead, that you are almost home and when you think back you will say 'How funny.' How sweet, yes, how sweet, that I was cold, that I felt frightened, that I wanted to be home, when we were almost there, and then that time had passed. I thought my mother will be at the bedside, you will be there, my husband. I will feel such love from all of you. I've had my child. Yes. It was not so bad, no. No, I was not frightened. Yes, I cried but no, I was not frightened, I had thought of this day a long time. A very long time. I would look into my husband's eyes. I never saw that look. Before or after, I would think. But yes, yes, that's what I anticipated. I knew it would be like this. Then I would sleep. Before I slept my mind would swim. What release! I would feel release, a long release. Yes, this is done, now this is finally done. I have had my child. I am delivered. I remember long ago. I thought of this. I always thought of this. One day he'll ask me, please, to tell him what it was like when he was born: I will tell him how it was. I thought he will be getting older. He will know certain questions about life, and this is what this means. Tell me about when I was born. And I will tell him how long I had wanted him, and the things I had thought. I'd think someday he'll tell this to *his* children. My god, I thought, he is growing up, is grown up. Is himself and formed, that time I thought that I was forming him, and he is formed already. *(Pause.)* I was deluding myself. And the time has passed. So quickly. And he is old now, I would think and he has his own life and his own questions. I would think I pray he does not hate me, I pray for those times when I have wronged him only through excess of love, I pray, but I knew that he would come to an understanding, to an understanding, someday, or he would forget in either case that it was passed, that he was grown, I felt remorse that he was grown. Could I not have anticipated this, I thought? It is so logical, I only had to look ahead, I thought, to see that he would grow. I thought, he will have children, how my mother must have thought this, one day she will have her own, and then she will know what I know. That old woman, who is she, I thought, your grandmother, I knew her when she still was young, once she was young like you, I thought, when I was walking in the snow, someday, how strange, how strange, but they will think that, someday they will be old, too, those pretty girls. Someday they will look like me, my son's girls, how my father would have liked them, I thought, someday he will feel remorse, someday he will look back. We should foresee these things, I thought, the rest is always passing, even while we think of it. Someday soon you will be grown. That's what I'd say to him, when he began to ask me, I would tell him stories. I'd say do you know when you were young I told you these same stories? Do you know? Do you remember? I'd say one day I was walking with my father in the woods. I was so cold. *(Pause.)* I was

9

very cold, I said, Papa, are we there? Are we almost there? And he said yes. *(Pause.)* Soon you will be sitting by the fire. Think you are thinking back to this time. It was almost done. And someday *you* can tell this story, I'd think, so I must remember it for you.

MONOLOGUE
(FEBRUARY 1990)

MONOLOGUE
(FEBRUARY 1990)

Who will read when I say who will read of who will hear
when I say that the thing was not the letter but a substance
on the cuff of my suede jacket which will not come off of
suede. It was a wax or plastic or the balled adhesive used in
envelopes. But such a profusion of it as could not come from
there. Not the portentous events or those whose demands ate
at the body constantly, so one could say, "It is ongoing, and
I am in control of it." While it made one ill. Those that one
says, speaking of them, "I am learning, I will learn, I have
learned, somewhat, to control my feelings, and act philosophi-
cally in deference to those things one can not change. For
why act otherwise, if one can not change them?" But, as one
can not, those several things, in their stead, or sent by our
concern for them, cognitive dissonance in all things, render-
ing us concerned with the arrangement of our clothes, when
we have gone sick in the aeroplane, and say, "this is one of
those times, when attendants will carry me out," and the attendants come to carry one, and one is just past saying, "No,
I can move on my own." For one can not move, and says of
the passengers, "now you have *your* world, and I have my *own*.
I am too sick to envy you. I am too sick for you to grudge
me the annoyance of the impediment I made to your trip."
Oh, let me go sick, then, and be relieved. When the cares of
the day, when the cares of the day become too heavy. Now,
reader, now, you have your own, your own letter, your own
suede jacket, your own little phrase, and this, which will or
will not put it in perspective — my troubles less than your
own, my joys greater than — to give you hope and envy. Un-

derstanding and forgiveness we must give ourselves — if that is what the letter said. What was the jacket for? What a jacket is for. The cuff, a pleasing distraction. Need not even be addressed. Save as a sign of change. Which we interpret as the punishment or the remission of a God whose personality differs from our own not at all. For Jesus wept as we weep. For our sins, which we either exult in full avowal of, or understand to be the fault of others. Jesus wept, and no one castigated you for being sick. There is that class of events of which one says this: If you were shamming, take it to the grave. And that is what the letter said. You bore the spot upon your cuff as the sign of a more hidden disfigurement, and it was in this that you found it pleasant to assert you knew not what the substance was, or who had caused it. In love of your unfathomable, infinitely extended mental processes. You saw that you had displaced that excuse inappropriate in any self-apology for the shameful but true accusations in the letter, on the condition of your cuff. But who would know, but those who read? And who would know they knew? And what would the broadcasting of your denial aid you in diminution of the shame you felt, for was it not all a rebuttal of a proposition the veracity of which you, in your conscious mind, embraced? Was there no end to them? No. There was no end to them. There was no where to turn. Dear reader, it is not you whom I elect to stand accomplice, but my viciously devious self, standing, as you, indeed, incapable of only those remonstrances which I assign to it — as an employee — it measures fulsome praise and credibility. And we exact, not the believability of the creation, but that the utterer exhausted his resources making the attempt.

TWO ENTHUSIASTS

TWO ENTHUSIASTS

A. For example, "All blue."

B. Yes.

A. Or "Coming on to final."

B. "Coming?"

A. "Turning?"

B. Turning...?

A. Turning, yes.

B. ... turn ...

A. "Turning."

B. "... just ..."

A. Just turning onto final.

B. *(Simultaneously with "Final"* "Turning onto final.") "The *Thresh* ..."

A. "Threshold of the Active."

B. *(Simultaneously with "Act.")* "Threshold of the Active."

A. Yes ...

B. The, what were we...?

A. "All blue."

B. "All bbbb ..." Or, "Read them." Or, "Read them and wwww ..." Oh oh. He said. "Yes, I ..."

A. When?

B. The other.

A. The last...?

B. Yes.

A. The ...

B. When I, I told you. Did.... Didn't I...?

A. *(Simultaneously with "I.")* The last one, you're...?

B. The other night.

A. "The other night," in fact.

B. "Sailed in a wooden shoe."

A. Sailed *off* in a *wooden shoe* ...

B.   Baseball.

A.   How could...?

B.   He *couldn't*, that's what I'm ...

A.   I suppose it's like *cricket.*

B.   Mmm.

A.   To us.

B.   Cricket to us. I kept, absolutely, I *told* myself ... I.... *Told* myself ... what was I? Where was I going? *(Pause.)* Where was I going? *(Pause.)* Paul ... *(Pause.)*

A.   Yes. *(Pause.)*

B.   Where was I going? *(Pause.)*

A.   We were discussing *cricket.* One of us averred, and who could we say it was *new,* for it is by no stretch, a novel observation.

B.   Cricket and ... cricket ...

A.   Cricket and ...

B.   *(Simultaneously with "And.")* Cricket and baseball are alike we shall say, for the purposes of this discussion. Hold it in your mind, the *topic.* Then, you know, the, *the* most perfect, *I think the most perfect* ... you know what I'm going to say...?

A.   Yes.

B.   You do?

A.   Yes.

B.   What am I going to say?

A.   You're going to say that the most perfect, the, Iambic Line, you're going to say — am I right?

B.   *Say* it.

A.   ... well, you *know* what I'm going to say.

B.   I do...?

A.   Yes.

B.   The, the ...

A.   ... he was discussing *baseball.*

B.   Rules, eh? Um, um, methods of *procedure.* All right.

A.   How could he fathom...?

B.   ... he could *not.* You'd say, well, *hell,* this is past where it is even interesting as *arcane.* All right, but *no, no, indeed,* and I was going to say "astounded me," but didn't astound me, but pleased me, as always *(Pause.)* in him. *(Pause.)* His interest.... You can't mark it up to, to, to, to, to.

A.   Academia.

B.   No, certainly not. Not ...

A.   "Certainly not, *'yes'* or *'no'*?"

B.   You *can't,* I'm saying, you can't mark it up.... "Mark it up?" "Chalk it up?" "Mark it off?"

A.   *"Write* it off...?"

B.   "Write it off," certainly, but, "mark it off?"

A.   "Sluff it off ..."

B.   "You can't chalk it up...?"

A.   "... you can't chalk it up...?"

B.   "You Can't Describe It *As* ... it's insufficient to describe it as an Academic Interest."

A.   ... grossly insufficient.

B.   As we know, *it goes beyond,* as I was saying ...

A.   It is *childlike.*

B.   That's the word.

A.   Isn't it?

B.   The word *itself* is childlike. *(Pause.)*

A.   Isn't it?

B.   Yes. *(Pause.)* Yes. It is. *(Pause.)* Yes.

A.   ... so warm ...

B.   And he said, "All right, then. The Pitcher Hits the Ball...?"

A.   ... not.

B.   ... not the Pitcher.

A.   All right. The:

B.   "The batter hits the ball" (That seems wrong, does it seem wrong, I don't know. Does it seem wrong? It seems wrong, but it's right.) "The people run around. And they run ..." Here he pauses. "And they run ... they run until ... well," he says, "They can't run *interminably. (Pause.)* No, you'll have to tell me."

A.   "You'll just have to tell me." *(Pause.)*

B.   "Isn't it...?"

A.   Yes. *(Pause.)*

B.   Hmmm. *(Pause.)*

A.   Hmmm.

B.   "You'll just have ..." *(Pause.)* "You'll just have ..." *(Pause.)*

"You'll just have to tell me." *(Pause.)* Turning on final.

A.   Turning *onto* final. Threshold of the active. And, you see, that's why, because "A *pallor* wreathed the *features* of the patrons of the game ..."

B.   And that's why?

A.   Arguably, yes. Because they have the same.... Do they have the same *sound?* Threshold pallor. Active features. Well, what matter, in a thousand years? None at all.

B.   None at all, at all.

A.   ... when we are dead and laid away.

B.   "... and no more privy to the sights and sounds..." "... and no more privy to the *weight* of sounds?"

A.   I would say so.

B.   "And ..." No, I've lost it. *(Pause.)*

A.   The pulsing light.

B.   What could it mean?

A.   It could mean, wait a minute, wait a moment, now, it could mean ...

B.   Div ...

A.   Divine ...

B.   Divine inter ...

A.   Not not not not ...

B.   *"Presence."*

A.   Presence, yes. Certainly. Certainly. It could mean ...

B.   You know, the thing about the *Martians* is that it just begs the question. One fellow told me he saw these lights at the end of the road, in the night, in the middle of the night. He saw them, in the midst of nowhere, in the woods. "What could they mean." Of *course,* but *meaning* that, if you will ...

A.   "Who made them."

B.   Of course.

A.   Although, if you would take that reductionist attitude, eh, why get up in the morning?

B.   Or, alternatively, be subsumed into the *Godhead.*

A.   If you will, but ...

B.   "The pulsing light."

A.   ... coming from the crib ...

B.   ... from the crib. All right, then; he was sleepy. He was *tired,* he was *overwrought.*

A.   "The difficulties of the last few days had left him drained."

B.   And, *drained ... (Pause.)* drained ... *(Pause.)* "*And,* drained, he was ..." *(Pause.)* "He was ..." *(Pause.)* "He was ..." Do you know, do you know, I was going to say, "It looked like vanilla" but it did *not* look like vanilla. "Then why was I going to say it?" And that is the central problem. *Isn't* it?

A.   It is "a" problem.

B.   Not the central problem, no. That is the central problem. If there ... *(Pause.)* It was *not* like vanilla, the important proportions of that color being that it *is* like vanilla. It is ... it is ... I saw in the paper where the High Court ruled, to the effect, much ... *literally* to the effect, in some ruling, that "'race' shall be." No, I excuse myself. That "Race" is held to mean "Race," and that "Color" to ... it went on, *Within the meaning of the law.*" And *Color,* or, "Within the meaning of *this* statute."

A.   Or "Within the meaning of *this* statute."

B.   "... to mean Color." Well, then. But it, for it, but it, and it *was* not like vanilla, being *unlike* vanilla in its ...

A.   ... tone and color.

B.   If you will; but a yellow, a sort of yellow, a weak yellow light. The *light* was yellow, I do not mean. I mean that the *color* was weak. But the *light* was strong. Not a lime, not canary, not, I wish I knew more names for it, but to what end, as all that I could use them for is to discard them. *How* can we say that is nothing, though? We cannot. We can say it, but it is not true. "A white light." ... "*Tinged* with yellow?" No. A strong ...

A.   Say, "An unearthly color."

B.   "... of a color ..." No, the color was not it. What I am *telling* you, and I know what he meant when he said, he, I beg your pardon, *without having said it,* what the color must have been. For it was not the thing, the, the, the ...

A.   Well, the *fact* of it must have been stupefying. *(Pause.)* Was it not, then?

B.   It was.

21

A. Well, say, "The color of surprise," and be damned to you.
B. For all time.
A. Or "Of the Gods."
B. ... with all my heart. The pulsing light. What could it mean? "Fall down and *worship* me, then, in a *mystery*." We say, for the worship of a *fact*, the worship of a *fact*. The worship of a fact must be idolatry. And ... and ...
A. You can "respect" a fact.
B. You can. But why?

SUNDAY AFTERNOON

SUNDAY AFTERNOON

A and B, two men. C, a woman.

At rise. A and B in a room.

A.   Other people could wear shorts, but I could not wear shorts.

B.   Why not?

A.   Because at one time I did not have the legs for it, and, as time passed, I developed, or perhaps I developed it quickly, which is to say, instantly, eh? As rationalization for my feelings that I was that I was that I was insufficient, if you follow me, perhaps most likely actually I first saw them and felt, How Ugly. The ugliness being, of course, in myself, and then as time went on I had identified the shorts as ugly and the *(Pause.)* the *hidden* feeling of shame at my legs persisted in my, my *rejection* of the shorts. Perhaps not. Perhaps that which persisted was my dislike of shorts. What do you think? Do you think: you see, not to say, not to say, that my dislike of them was not was not not not, that it was "healthy," but the ... *be* it, if it were, neurotic, which is to say not founded on axia which, if brought to the light would reflect my own assessment of my own best interests ... where was I? That if it were so, still it might be different than my need to *(Pause.)* my need to ritualize my own shamed feeling at my ugly legs, my own election that I was no good, that I was not a good person, that I was a bad person, that I was deserving of nothing, you see, no *love*, no sex, no ... no ... *peace*, finally, no no consideration. That I was "bad." We see these things, we see them in others. Can we not can we not be compassionate? The criminal, perhaps, who would, or the rude person in the street, or in the restaurant; who would behave in such a way were it not for a feeling of self-loathing, which caused him to see a world which was not there, in which, in fact, everything that he saw was a reiteration of that central theme of his own loathsome state, of his obscenity. And after they are ritualized, how can we extract them, for we do not know that they exist. Then how can we extract them?

B.   I ...

A.   *(Simultaneously with "I.")* I'm sorry...?

B.   Go ahead. I'm sorry. Go ahead. Please.

A.   I'm sorry. Go ahead. Please.

B.   No, go on.

A.   All right. *(Pause.)* What was I going to say? You know. Tell me. What was I going to say?

B.   ... something to the ...

A.   ... something ...

B.   ... something to the point of planets.

A.   Absolutely right.

B.   It is?

A.   Like the misunderstanding of the Northern Lights. Not not the, no, not, not ...

B.   The meteor.

A.   The meteor that night. The meteorite. Yes. It *struck* me, you know, in a book, how you could draw a line, trace a line from one to the next, of the constellations. In the sky, also, you could do it, later I saw why not, for *they are fixed*, of course. They are fixed.

B.   Yes.

A.   ... fixed in their relation to each other. As, of course, they have to be. *If* they are fixed, then their relations can be simply charted. Ah *ha,* ah *ha,* ah *ha.* Yes. But that's the *stars.* In our geometry — I was going to say, like the *planets,* that we do not *see* them, but from the pull they exert, then we must posit their existence. Do you see?

B.   ... we do not see them ...

A.   You know what I mean.

B.   The ones we do not see.

A.   Yes. Ones we do not see, or have not seen, ones we may see now because our "optics" ... *(Pause.)* If you will. But heretofore we could not see them, and ones, I believe, which we come we come to suspect, whose orbit, I believe it is possible, *fixes* them behind a larger body. Do you see, so that its relative position to our eyes is hidden. How could we see that?

B.   And such a thing would exert a pull on our world.

A.   Aha. Perhaps. Perhaps not, perhaps not on our, well, well, or *some* world. *Some* world ... I know. Its *"mass"* or whatever it is, would, don't you see, alter the progression of something ... the world which *hid* it, certainly, or ... and I believe that one affects, that one affects the other, so on. Must it not, must it not, then, devolve to ... *(Pause.)* It affects the universe in which we live. So with neurosis, must it not control; or the man *obsessed* with that star. You, perhaps, or myself, obsessed with the existence, yea or nay, of your will, of that star, who'd spend a life, who ...

B.   ... but in our case it is just the reverse.

A.   It is?

B.   Yes.

A.   What is the reverse?

B.   One who had seen the pull and reasoned backward to ... to the "necessity" of a star, you say, to ... of a body in that place.

A.   And that is the reverse?

B.   Yes. *(Pause.)*

A.   The reverse of what?

B.   You said. A man who strove to prove there was a star there. And I said a man who perceived a force and sought it till he posited that its exclusive source could be, solely, this body to which we've referred. *(Pause.)* This hidden body. *(Pause.)*

A.   ... this hidden body, then ...

B.   ... yes.

A.   Yes, *what?*

B.   Yes ... *(Pause.)* Yes, there was a hidden body.

A.   Where?

B.   Where?

A.   Yes, well, in our conversation, surely, not to be facetious.

B.   ... no ...

A.   ... but that we referred to it.

B.   ... yes.

A.   Always ... always ... *(Pause.)* such power. *(Pause.)* Such power. Power such that though we strive to break from it, that though we strive, as we do, in our lives, as we do, do we not, and is it not the central and the unifying *theme* of our lives, that which we deny ... the very strife does homage to it, does it not? It screams its existence to a world which, as it lives behind the other thing, was unaware of it. God damn me, then, for a conceited fool to think I could escape from it, and even *that* an homage to the secret thing. How can we know it? And if it is removed, then ... *(Enter C.)*

B.   If it is removed, then what? *(Pause.)*

A.   Then what.

B.   Yes.

A.   *(To C.)* How are you?

C.   I'm fine.

B.   If it is removed, then what?

A.   *(To C.)* What is it?

C.   I cut myself.

A.   How?

C.   In the kitchen.

A.   With a knife?

C.   Yes.

A.   Are you all right?

C.   I don't know. I got all giddy.

A.   Is it bleeding? Let me see it.

C.   It was bleeding, and I put a bandage on it.

A.   Is it bleeding now?

C.   I think it is.

B.   Let me see it.

C.   I stuck it in my mouth.

A.   Does it hurt?

C.   No.

A.   Is it a deep cut? May I ask you to let me see it again?

C.   I, I don't want to take the bandage off.

A.   Did you wrap it so that it, so that it won't stick? I should see it.

C.   I don't want to take it off. You know ... I think that it
will heal. What were you talking of? You know, though, the
thing of it is my first thought was thank God that I was not
a man, you know? In war. Because I, what do they say? Went
all giddy.

B.   ... went all queer.

C.   I went all queer, I got lightheaded. I'm sure that that's
what that means. As if I'd lost a lot of blood, I *did* lose quite
a lot of blood. "How much blood did you lose?" Well, it's
hard to tell when it's yours — it starts bleeding, you know ...
when it's really bleeding ...

B.   ... yes ...

C.   And that's your *life* flowing out of you, then, *innnit?* You
see, I was *making the fucking lunch* ... don'tcha know ... *(Pause.)*

B.   I think that I should see it.

C.   It was of that order where ... *(Pause.)* so rare nowadays,
actually, I aver. Which did not admit of interpretation. Which
is to say it was something which had actually occurred. I'm all
right. It was just that I became frightened because I thought
I was going to die. I think I'm frightened.

B.   Something like that would scare anyone. *(He looks at the
wound.)*

C.   Well, that's the thing I *thought* of, you see: when I
thought "you coward ... not only are you *dying,* not only are
you clumsy and have *killed* yourself, but *here's* something you
didn't know: you are a coward."

B.   You're saying because you were not inured to the
blood...?

C.   I ruined the bloody fucking ham.

B.   I think you should have this looked at.

A.   You bled on it?

C.   ... in what way...? Stitches...? Stitches...? Cleansing...?

B.   Yes.

C.   I let it bleed, though.

B.   ... to cleanse it...?

C.   Yes. To cleanse it. And ...

B.   ... you stuck it in your mouth.

C.   Yes. And I ran it underneath the cold water.

B.   Uh huh. Did you see, was there ... what what what what were you cutting? You were cutting the ham.

C.   Yes.

B.   With that knife.

C.   I was cutting the ham with the knife. I cut my thumb with ... *(Pause.)* Ah ah ... was ... is there, I suppose there is, is there ... you are cutting *"meat"* ...

A.   The question is: although we *eat* it, is there that in meat which, transmitted otherwise than through digestion, that is it say, uhhhh, directly, to the blood, can ...

B.   Yes, or particles ...

A.   Cause infection.

B.   ... the presence of a foreign object.

A.   ... *I think so.*

B.   I think so, too.

C.   I was cutting the ham, I washed the knife ...

B.   ... yes ...

C.   and I ...

A.   No, I can't think that it makes a difference if it was washed, when the question is if it was sterilized.

B.   Well, then, let's take her in. I'm serious. Let's do it.

C.   Oh, Christ, you know, I feel so ... I ... on *top* of it, and then feeling "giddy" ...

B.   You're feeling giddy now?

C.   Yes.

B.   Come on, I'm going to take you in. *(Bustles about and exits.)*

C.   *(To A.)* Why did you ask me if I bled on it? *(Pause.)*

A.   If ...

C.   Why did you ask me if I bled on the ham?

A.   Why do you think? Because I wanted to know ... I ... I wanted to know if we could eat it. Do you know what I'd just thought of?

C.   No.

A.   The African Woman that time.

B.   *(Entering.)* I'm going to call the doctor. *(Exits.)*

A.   That African Woman that time.

C. Uh huh.

A. Are you uncomfortable?

C. Yes.

A. With her bowl of porridge. How is your hand? I don't mean porridge. What do I mean?

C. Stew.

A. Why did I say "porridge?"

C. Because you said "bowl."

A. How is your hand?

C. I think that I am going to be fine. I would like a drink.

A. Mm hmm.

C. You think that's contraindicated?

A. No.

C. Please?

A. Scotch.

C. Please.

A. Mmm.

C. What did she do?

A. She made us the stew.

C. I don't remember.

A. Yes, you do.

C. In Africa.

A. In Boston.

C. Because, yes, I do remember in Boston, an African woman, but I don't remember Africa, you see, and I got frightened.

A. I understand.

C. I thought: funny thing about it, you know, funny thing: it all goes out the window, when you're panicked. You say "I am now in an animal state." Well, *fuck* it. Anything can put you there. I *knew* I'd never been to Africa. Tell me. What did she do?

A. You remember her.

C. She served us stew. She ... what? She ... she.... What did she do?

A. We all ...

C. We all ... ah ah ah ah ah we were sitting in a *circle* and

31

we had to *eat it with our hands.*

A. Out of the bowl.

C. Out of the *One Big Bowl* ... and you said that was the most difficult thing you had ever done.

A. It was.

C. It was the most difficult thing you had ever done. And you were *talking* ... you were *talking* of the ham. How ... no no no, you won't offend me, how ... how you must have felt so ... what what ... "cowardly." No. What? Yes. Such a simple thing ... and you'd say, "I have done such ... much more intimate things ... intimate things with her." *(He hands her a drink.)* On the other hand ... *(Of drink.)* Thank you.

A. Drink it. *(Pause.)*

C. Ah, fuck, I don't care anymore.

B. *(Reentering.)* Can you see bone; did it hit the bone; is it clean ... has ... *(Pause.)*

A. "Has the bleeding stopped?"

B. No ... has ... *(Pause.)*

A. "Has ..."

B. ... wait wait ... oh hell ...

C. Are you no good in emergencies?

B. ... well, that would account for it ... but ... uh.... Ah Ah! Have you ...

C. *(Getting up.)* Well, let *me* fucking talk to him. *(Exits.)*

A. Did he seem concerned? *(Pause.)* Did the doctor seem concerned? Hello. *(Pause.)* Had she been "vaccinated?"

B. *Vaccinated!* Yes! Had she had tetanus ...

A. Well, good.

B. And there was another thing.

A. I was saying I got so *squeamish* ... and I felt so *cowardly,* you know ...

B. No, I don't know.

A. Because ...

B. Why?

A. Well, I'm telling you ...

B. Because you didn't, um, you didn't want to eat the ham.

A. And I thought what a bloody fucking *waste,* you know?

More than the ham. Because she put me *off* ham.

B.   Um hmm.

A.   And I had been looking forward to it.

B.   Understandable.

C.   *(Entering.)* Have I been vaccinated?

B.   ... *(To A.)* What did I tell you!

END

THE JOKE CODE

THE JOKE CODE

A.   ... but, you know, what I want is Wisdom.

B.   Then where will you get it? *(Pause.)* Where can it be got? *(Pause.)* Where is it to be got? Except in Longing?

A.   ... in Longing, certainly.

B.   ... where is it to be got, except in longing? *(Pause.)* In empty pages. *(Pause.)* More wisdom *there* ... *(Pause.)* Mmmm?

A.   Yes.

B.   Something on your mind.

A.   Yes.

B.   ... in longing, or in ... *(Pause.)* What was I saying? *Wisdom.* Death. Death, certainly — or any Miracle. You can, you can, I firmly believe this, I, I know it to be true, that you can *do* it: in it, it is like technique — that you can *do* it when you no longer, or you could say that you can only embrace its true *nature* ... eh ...

A.   ... yes ...

B.   ... *when you no longer require (Pause.)* If I may ... *(Pause.)* Or, to put it differently, when its dross purpose no longer *(Pause.) When You No Longer Need It.* And I think ... *(Pause.)* Yes, yes, you're right.

A.   I am right in...?

B.   In that that is the purpose of any technique.

A.   ... that I was thinking that...?

B.   Yes.

A.   ... Mmm.

B.   To, would you say, we could say, to, yes, it *is* sad to say it, but we must say it; for it is true. And I ... "To *grow* sad ..." To wean ourselves. To, to, to, to ...

A.   To school ourselves.

B.   To, yes. It is. To school ourselves in sadness. Well, you know, you could say, "Oh, the *sadness* of it all." But *like* — what do you think, eh? —

A.   Well, tell me.

B.   *Like* the Miracle. Or "like," or "not *un*like ..." But more, yes, *like* the ... *(Pause.)* Mmm.

A.   You were saying "sadness"...?

B.   And I thought that *like* the *(Pause.)* I'm sorry. You said something was on your mind. What was it? You seem distrait. I had the mere minimum to, good grace to, *absent* hypocrisy in not waiting your *answer. Ask* you ... but you seem distrait.

A.   "What is it"...?

B.   Yes.

A.   Nothing.

B.   A certain "heaviness?"

A.   If you will.

B.   Aha.

A.   And then you were saying:

B.   That *like* to the Miracle, if still are wed to the *effect* of it, you cannot *do* it. If you are free of the drug of its *appearance* — which way should you grasp it? It is not miraculous because you can *accomplish* it, and, so, it is commonplace, *or* — are they the same thing? I think they are. Am I embarrassing myself? I think that they are the same thing.

A.   The other being?

B.   That we can *accomplish* it only having forsworn, beyond 'forsworn,' whatever ... renounced? No. Whatever that Eastern State ...

A.   To "exist independently of"?

B.   Perhaps. Yes. Perhaps. *(Pause.)* Which — doesn't it? — Seems so mundane to *say* it. N'we could say The Phrase Itself Negates the Possibility Of — you see ...

A.   Yes.

B.   If we could *posit* it (except that it does not) or what, eh, what even then the ... what was the question? *(Pause.)* We spoke of sadness. "Finally, then, sadness is sad." Well, yes. "Finally, then, to *say* it is sad is to ..." Aha ... something ... something ... *(Pause.)* I asked you if — I saw that you were blue. I asked, I said, I saw that I had ... *(Pause.)* I saw that I

38

had acted hypocritically: perhaps not hypocritically, yes, hypo-critically. If we cannot *"name"* things, then ... *(Pause.)* What? *(Pause.)* Does it mean that we cannot *talk* of them? *(Pause.)* Well, we cannot *say* them, then, certainly, and must say that *that* is to-the-good — I think — But can we feel them? Yes. Although we may say, certainly, that there are those things: feelings, shades ... *(Pause.)* Shades of feelings, feelings them-selves, possibly, (I think so) which we could not experience if we had not *named* them. Leaving to debate whether, if you will, we are better off *before* having possessed those feelings, most of which, perhaps I am wrong, those exquisite ...

A.   ... graduations ...

B.   ... if you will ... seem to do with melancholy.

A SCENE – AUSTRALIA

A SCENE – AUSTRALIA

Two women. A and B.

A.   Who would have thought he was the kind of person who would take his bride into my mother's shop, dress her up in *all* sorts of finery, move to Australia, and then murder her. Her *and* the kids. *Now,* mind you, he's in the, he's in the blah blah Tasmania, some minimum, or, no, I don't know, security, some prison, a workfarm there; he commutes, that's not the word, with *Princeton,* he communicates on the same, on the, well, why *shouldn't* he, on the same, on the very problems ... but why *should* he? On the other hand.

B.   How does he do it?

A.   By computer. But it makes you *question.* If you ask yourself, what is the *purpose,* 'cause it's either *wrong* or *right,* I think, to deprive someone of their liberty. As he ...

B.   ... yes.

A.   ... *as* he did to them.

B.   And as we do to him.

A.   In a way. Yes, in a way either *more* or *less* ... *(Pause.)* More, either *more* or *less* ...

B.   ... terrible.

A.   ... thank.... Thank you ...

B.   ... than he did to them.

A.   And where is the right? *Or* ... *(Pause.)* or either or it's *right* he stays in prison, and he lives his life; or ...

B.   Or it's wrong ...

A.   Or it's wrong. And I Do Not Know. I don't know the answer. Some times I come down on prejudice, on, on the side of prejudice, and say one thing, and say "vengeance." Some days I say "judge not," and then I think it's coddling.

Not that I think of it so *often*, but to've been in close *proximity* ... he asked me out.

B. He didn't.

A. Yes. He did. Oh. Yes, he did. He asked me out. I could have gone with him. My mother said "go with him."

B. Why didn't you?

A. I didn't like him. I could say that I knew something ... who *knows* if I did? He asked me to the movies, and it could of been I didn't like the *film; although* I seem to see that, *yes,* I didn't like the film, but *I didn't like him!* And then I think ...

B. ... yes?

A. *Would* it of been, had I been a, *thinking* about it, all I can think, I had been a *whore* to go with him *because I liked the movie,* with a boy I didn't *like,* what would of *happened* to mẹ! I could of ended *marrying* the boy, *and* moving, *and* being killed, I think, as a punishment ... *I* understand it. Say it's harsh, it's *beyond* harsh. It *is* harsh. It's *hard.* But On Some Level ... I, *Myself, I* understand it, had I *sacrificed* myself ...

B. ... uh huh ...

A. ... to go with him, *because* I liked the film ... *(Pause.)* Had I ... had, had I *done* that ...

B. ... you can't blame yourself.

A. ... and then I say "saved my chance"

B. "Saved by Chance" ...

A. Yes. Because I wasn't *tested.*

B. ... be ...

A. ... because I didn't like the *film*. His *other* wife, not, not his other wife ...

B. his "wife" ...

A. ... his "wife" ... was she, in some way ... not, "for going to a *movie* ..." But ...

B. ... yes ...

A. ... for ...

B. ... for not being "true" to herself ...

A. for not being "true" to herself. Was she *killed,* you see, you see, for making that *one step,* which was a wrong step, which she made *when she knew she should not,* and one thing

44

led on, and it led *on,* and on, and she's married to a *psychopath,* and ... and, you see, in that last moment before the knife fell, and, thinking: "I knew this was wrong from the first moment." *(Pause.)*

B. Maybe she liked the film. *(Pause.)*

A. Well, all right. Of course. Yes. And maybe she liked the *guy,* and maybe she liked all the things that *happened* to her. Maybe we *all* do. But I Don't Think So. And I think we always know. And I think that she knew in that first moment, and I say God *Damn* him, for he could of just left her alone, and now he's living in some *"place,"* and now she's dead, and it seems to me that vast *movements* have taken place, and I can't figure it out, perhaps you can explain it to me.

FISH

FISH

Two men.

A.   The, the, then, when the angel came to him, it wasn't an angel, what was it, a fish, a devil, or ...

B.   ... some representative.

A.   That's right. Of ...

B.   ... some power.

A.   ... that power, some power, that power, yes. It was ... what difference, really, right?

B.   That's right.

A.   If we examine it.

B.   That's right.

A.   Don't you think?

B.   Yes.

A.   ... when it *came* to him — for, of *course*, it must be the same power ...

B.   Of course it is.

A.   And even if you split it in two parts...

B.   Yes.

A.   ... when it *came* to him ... does this disturb you?

B.   No.

A.   ... it said: "You have ..." whatever ... what did I say? Why did I say it's a fish?

B.   Be ...

A.   ... that's another one, right?

B.   Right.

A.   Where a fish comes from the sea...

B.   ... that's right.

A.   Yes, and demands three wishes. He ... *I'm* sorry. The fish, the ...

B.   The fish *grants* the wishes.

A.   The fish *grants* the wishes. In *this* it's the *Devil. That's* who it is. *I* knew who it was. It ...

B.   It's the Devil.

A.   *I* know who it is. He comes in guises of a *farmer.* He says ... why did I forget him?... "I will give you Gold beyond your wildest dream." (Or things which the Hearer wants.) I'm not even sure it *was* gold. It probably was gold. It makes no difference. It's something which makes no difference. How many times one has thought, in dreams or waking, "If I *were* to die, how differently I would live this day." The *Devil* says, "I'll give you Gold ..." or whatever then, or, in the story, he comes to some man ...

B.   ... yes ...

A.   ... who's in *extremity;* and he, Ah! He, he says, "I know your problem: what would you give me if I could *fix* it?" "Anything." "So. I will *trade* you five years, ten years, whatever" ... he makes a bargain, "in exchange for your immortal soul." It *occurred* to me: What the Bargain *is:* finally, what I think, the *bargain* is, is not in the *gold,* but in the years of life. *(Pause.)*

B.   Of course.

A.   Yes see what I mean?

B.   Yes.

A.   You agree?

B.   Yes. Why did you say it was a farmer?

A.   I remember that it was.

B.   When?

A.   Long ago, I heard it.

B.   What was it?

A.   A proverb.

B.   When did you hear it?

A.   Oh, *you* know, long ago.

B.   In childhood?

A.   Yes.

B.   And the man asked for Gold?

A.   I don't know. I don't think so.

B.   No. I didn't either.

A.   I know that he didn't ask for Gold.

B.   What did he ask for?

A.   Some things *stay* with you; and I've found that they reoccur, at different times in your life, in differing shapes. *Finally; finally,* (Pause.) Yes. *Finally* the man that *came,* The *Devil* said: "You must grant me three wishes." *(Pause.)* "Grant me three wishes and then you can die." That's what I think. Why should I be ashamed of that? Don't you think? *(Pause.)* Don't you think?

B.   No. I think that's very good.

A.   And *that* was my confusion.

B.   Yes. I understand.

A.   Not the *"fish"* ...

B.   I totally und ...

A.   Not the fish at all. Oh, good. *(Pause.)* "Grant me."

B.   I understand. It's all right.

A.   *(Pause.)* "Grant me ..." *(Pause.)* "Grant me these three wishes." "Grant me these three wishes." *(Pause.)* "Grant me these three wishes, I will set you free."

A PERFECT MERMAID

A PERFECT MERMAID

A.   "My luck: the perfect mermaid. Not only did she have the *tail* of a fish ..."
B.   "the bottom ...?"
A.   The bottom?
B.   "The bot ..."
A.   "... not only ..."
B.   "the tail ...?"
A.   "Not only did she ..." I don't know — "Not only did she ..." What did I...? "The bottom ..." All right. "*My* luck ..." "The tail?"
B.   "... the tail ..."
A.   *"Not Only Did She ..."*
B.   "... my luck ..."
A.   "My luck, the Perfect Mermaid ..."
B.   "Met her on the beach ..."
A.   I don't, no ... I don't think so. Well. Well. "Walking on the beach." "My luck." "The Perfect Mermaid. *Not only did she ...*"
B.   "Possess?"
A.   *"Not Only Did She Possess* the ..." There's your problem.
B.   "Not only did she possess ... the *Tail* of a fish ..."
A.   "A Fish's tail."
B.   "She had a ..." "Well, we beat you there."
A.   The Perfect Mermaid.
B.   "So She Said."
A.   Alrr ...   "She said she was the perfect mermaid."
B.   "... walking on the Beach ..."
A.   "I'm walking on the beach, I met ..."
B.   What.
A.   Yes. Yes.
B.   Who.
A.   Who ... I met a ... woman...?

B.   I met ... *someone...?*

A.   Walking on the beach, she claimed she was

A and B.   *(Simultaneously.)* The Perfect Mermaid. *(Pause.)* Not only ...

A.   Did she possess ...

B.   *(Simultaneously with above .)* Did she have.... She had the *tail* of a fish?

A.   *(Simultaneously with "tail.")* Not only did she possess the *tail* of a fish.

B.   ... she had a fish's head.

A.   How did it go?

B.   On the beach, walking on the beach. She claimed ...

A.   She told me that she was ...

B.   "She told me that she was ..."

A.   Rrr ... or ... or! Or! We could *posit,* therefore ...

B.   "... just my luck ..."

A.   "You want to think *that* way ..."

B.   ... I'm with you.

A.   *(Simultaneously with "you.")* "The perfect *mermaid* would possess, not only,"

B.   ... not ...

A.   Yes, yes. "Not only would possess the *bottom...?*"

B.   ... bot ...

A.   "A fish's *tail,* but would possess a fish's head, too." No. No. *(Pause.)*

B.   "If you ..." No. Um. "You want to take *that* attitude ..."

A.   No no no no no no no no. "I'm walking. On the beach. I met a *mermaid.* Just my *luck* ..."

B.   Yes.

A.   *"Not only does she ..."*

B.   ... possess the body of a fish ...

A.   "She had the head of a fish, too." *(Pause.)* Too. *(Pause.)* Yes?

B.   I'm walking.

A.   On the beach.

B.   I meet a mermaid. She tells me that she's a mermaid. No no no. No. "Walking on the" ... yes ... yes ...

A.   "Walking on the beach. I meet a mermaid. Just my luck.

Not only does she have the body of a fish. She has the head of a fish, too."

B.   "So perfectly equipped ..."

A.   No. No. *(Pause.)* No. *(Pause.)* No.

B.   "And just my luck."

A.   "Down the hill from the *blah* blah house ..."

B.   The Mansion House.

A.   "The clapboard ..." all right, but the clapboard house, not clapboard, shingled, though ...

B.   Not a romantic word.

A.   No.

B.   "Brooding"

A.   No.

B.   ... som ...

A.   No.

B.   Somber.

A.   "Porched." Something like, porti ...

B.   "Porticoed"

A.   But no.

B.   "Down the hill ..."

A.   Down the hill from the ...

B.   What is it? It is *old*, it's brooding, not so friendless, so foreboding, though. It's *dark*, it comes to.

A.   Yes.

B.   Life only in the Summer.

A.   It now is...?

B.   It now is Autumn.

A.   "The ..." *(Pause.)*

B.   Yes. *(Pause.)*

A.   "And. Cold. Winds. Blow."

B.   "Not so ..."

A.   Yes. "Not so chilly, though, as ... as ..."

B.   That's the problem of the house.

A.   "As ..."

B.   Warning ...

A.   *Say* it.

B.   *"Warning."*

A.   ... gently warning ...

B. ... winds?

A. "The *stately* house?" "Adumbrate Towr'd Above the Sand ..."

B. "The house sat up there ..." *How* is it...?

A. "Down the hill from the House Above." Well, there you have it. "Walking on the beach he encountered a mermaid. *So perfectly formed,* not *only* did she." Oh fuck. "Not ..." *(Pause.)* "So perfectly formed that not only did she possess the tail of a fish, she had a fish's head, too." "A fish's head?"

B. She *had a fish* head, *too.*

A. "She had ..."

B. And life flows past us.

A. Life. Life flows past us, he thought. "The house." "Times when he." "Times in the past." "Magic fish." The ...

B. ... you cannot say ...

A. I cannot...?

B. "Flotsam and jetsam."

A. "Rubbish of the sea...?"

B. "Washed forward on the land. Only to be ..."

A. Yes. Yes. Yes. *Toyed* with it.

B. Yes.

A. Pushed it forward.

B. Yes. They did.

A. Only to tease it back.

B. Tantalum.

A. So pre ...

B. So pre ... cocious?

A. Precarious.

B. Tentative? No.

A. Tenuous. Grip on the marge ...

B. It was a *fish,* is what it was — fuck was it doing *talking?*

A. Did it talk?

B. "Met a fish. So perfectly formed." Not only ... claimed, claimed, how did he know?

A. "Just my luck ..."

B. "It claimed to *be* a mermaid?"

A. "Just my luck. I met a mermaid on my walk."

B. Did it talk? Uh uh uh ... an *elective* ... a *putative.* A ... "I saw a fish," then ...

A.   "Down the hill from the house." "Head of a man, body of a man ..."

B.   That's right.

A.   The *Silky*.

B.   Cast himself into the sea? He *could*. He had the attributes. How did he *not*? While, on the land, to stand as Human. All observers — not to say him Nay.

A.   "However"...?

B.   Though on the sandy Marge, his love ... A fish...? "Best of the mer ..." Merwomen?

A.   Mermaids.

B.   Silly of me. Waiting. Waiting. "To his ... *oceanic*...?"

A.   Certainly not.

B.   "To his *sea-eyes* ..."

A.   Amen.

B.   "The perfection of form."

A.   ... head of a fish, body of a fish.

B.   It was a fish.

A.   "*Down* the hill from the house. Saw a fish. *Lapped* by the brine. Teased. Forward and teased back.

B.   Expiring?

A.   "Watched it resumed by the sea ..."

B.   ... my soul.

A.   Oh, my soul.

B.   "Etched in salt. Then eaten. And he never knew. He never saw it. *(Pause.)* It never happened. There was no house. *(Pause.)* We were not here. We were here, but we never spoke. We spoke of other things." *(Pause.)*

A.   We were not here, but it *was* a fish?

B.   "The ..." *(Pause.)* "The *head* of a fish ..."

A.   "The head of a fish, the *body* of a fish ..."

B.   "The perfection of form."

A.   Oh, just one word, then, before we retire.

B.   "That, of a certainty, things had occurred. He did not know them. We cannot be certain of their import, though we know ..."

A.   ... the Land, the Water ...

B.   ... though we know ... "Though, of a certainty, we can as-
sert the following, and hold it to be true. As long as we shall
find it pleasant. We:"
A.   "These things, then ..."
B.   "*Happy* men."
A.   ... That's right.
B.   Content.
A.   *Happy* men. Strength and Union.
B.   What is beauty, then, but this?

END

DODGE

DODGE

Two men.

An old man and younger man.

A.   The reason that they had those, you would say, "nick-names": man came into town you didn't ask him where he's from, you didn't ask him ...
B.   What his name was.
A.   That's right. You did not. And so, you would say, a *culture* sprung up of the custom to assign a man a name based on some aspect of, well, let's say his *behavior*. So they, what they would, you see, that in itself would reinforce the thing that what's important in a man is the way he comports himself.

A man once wrote that countries where the populace is armed people tend to be more polite. I think that's true, and you may say it is a ruse, or Southern Honor is a pleasant fiction, but I've found it true — and, past a point, people *do* act the way they've learned is expected of them. So there's some good in it in any case. Now: men who fall afoul of the law. Some men seek for that; perhaps you'd say by birth, by training, by inclination — but however it is so, and there are bad men in the world, though it pains me to say it, and I did not always hold it true. How does one deal with them?

They must be dealt with strongly.

First thing is to know them, and one can shun them with-out the taint of cowardice, as one would shun a pest, or predator. For one could deal with them, but why seek trouble if one has the choice. If you must go, then be direct. For bad men will interpret courtesy as weakness. *When* your paths cross, make it clear you do not intend to be trifled with, and book no disrespect, if he is going to erupt, as he will, let him take himself off and do it elsewhere.

For the man who says it's his responsibility to cleanse the blot the bad man represents, that man's a bully, too, and a self-righteous one. And I've an example of *that* which I will tell you later.

In countries where the men are armed, the saying is it's better to be judged by twelve than carried by six. So from the moment when you *decide* to go for your gun do not hesitate until your man is dead.

In Dodge there lived a man whom we called Mike, or Pennsylvania Mike, although he did not come from that state, or we had no reason to believe he did — for this is how those names arose. He'd done something ... *(Pause.)* No, I tell a lie: Keystone Mike. *Keystone,* for ... for, yessir! He'd sat down, there was a poker game at some, at, it escapes me, some resort, each day at one-o'clock they would sit down, this man played in that game, he was a regular. One day, the players were short, this man had absented himself, and there were only three, which is a languid game, to while away the hours, for, hand-by-hand, it is always two-on-one, two against one, one way or the other. And Mike was a high-player and, so a favorite. So this day he was absent and the game dragged. When he, when he made his entrance, he pulled up his chair to that three-handed contest and the dealer said "Here is the keystone of our game." *(Pause.)* ... here is the keystone of our game. So "Keystone Mike." And, jocularly, once in a while, perhaps, "Keys," and so I must suppose, *although* I misremembered it, for his name *was* "Keystone," that one might have referred to the man, with that passion which we all possess for elaboration, as "Pennsylvania."

He lived in Dodge in that time I'm referring to, when it was Railhead for the Cattle Drive, or, as I've read in books, although I cannot *remember* hearing it called so, "The End of Steel." Who could of called it that?

Near eighty-thousand head of cattle for transshipment, in Dodge, quite a lot of money. As I said, he was the Keystone, wore a fob on his waist of a .45 Long Colt, you know they say the *Indians,* their pagan, what we might call "medicine," which we take to mean their "religion," one aspect, a sort of magazine they carried of those things, those things that had *affected* them. In dreams, or visions: in their lives. They wore a medicine bag, and it contained beads, say, or the hoof of a doe, a shell, hair of a vanquished adversary (in those times gone by) things which both had meaning in their eyes and supernatural weight. And we might say "benighted as Egyptians in their Fog," but working through my *own* pockets I'd find, I'd find, in my own pockets I would find, a Walking Liberty Half Dollar, the shell of a .32 Long Colt ... and there's a story to *those* things. *(Pause.)*

B.   You said a most peculiar thing.

A.   I?

B.   In his pocket.

A.   When he *died* ...

B.   You were speaking of *totems.*

A.   It has *fascinated* me, how things arrive in books. Misinformation. Fellow knows the way it's done, community, man comes in, one day, part of a day, writes a book, you understand me? Which *traduces* that ...

B.   ... knowledge.

A.   That knowledge, yes. And then ... *(Pause.)* And then ... you find it in a book, it's not, you see, it's like a gunfight, one man walks away, the *book* becomes the record. After men have died. For the *Men* ... *(Pause.)* The men ... *(Pause.)*

B.   ... the men are dead.

A.   And it is foolish to rail, at the way of the world. *(Pause.)* At the way of Gods, for, certainly, there are things, are *meant* to be lost. For if they weren't *meant* to be lost why are they so? And that man wasn't worse, some worse, I'll say it, much worse than the rest of us? No. I'll say "No."

B.   And he had in his pocket?

A.   The story is this: a woman he'd insulted. Threw a flowerpot at him — he's seated, with his back to her. He rose to turn and drew his gun. The chair skid under him, he went down. And he shot himself. And died. Inside his pocket, in the pocket of his vest, found ivory baby beads, on which the name was written "Clement." What a marvelous country!

L.A. SKETCHES

L.A. SKETCHES

Scene 1

A.   Don't let him bulldoze you. Go *in* there, tell him what — get it? *Tell* him, you *tell* him ... what do you want? Fifty? *(Pause.)* What? Fifty?

B.   Seventy-five.

A.   That's what you're asking? Seventy-five?

B.   Yeah.

A.   Okay.

B.   You think it's too high?

A.   No.

B.   You think I'm too high.

A.   No. *(Pause.)* No. *(Pause.)* What would you take? *(Pause.)* Sixty? *(Pause.)*

B.   I ...

A.   I don't mean to *insult* you. I figure you said seventy-five you'd take seventy. I mean, you aren't going to blow it over five grand. I mean ... you aren't going to blow it over five grand ... I'm thinking, all I'm thinking is the way *he'd* think. You tell him seventy-five he'll think, "He says seventy-five he'd take seventy, so that's the top I have to go. How low would he go? Sixty ... fifty...?" *(Pause.)*

B.   I think it's worth seventy-five.

A.   Then that's what you should ask for.

B.   Should I ask for more to *get* the seventy-five?

A.   What can you ask for? You come in too *high,* he's going to think you're bluffing and come back too low. What would you *take?*

B.   Sixty.

A.   You'd take sixty?

B.   Yes.

69

A.   Would you ... all right: what you *got:*

B.   I think it's worth seventy-five, I'd *take* sixty. I don't want to put myself in a position where I have to *fight* from sixty.

A.   No. I understand that. No. What you have ... I'm thinking like him ...

B.   Yes.

A.   What you have to do is set a bottom ... like in *Vegas.* You've got to say *absolutely* how low you won't go beneath, and go from ... *reason* to that point, to what you want the ...

B.   ... I know that ...

A.   ... what you want the final figure ...

B.   ... I know that ...

A.   ... I know you do.... The final price to be.

B.   I know that. *(Pause.)* You think I should tag that at fifty?

A.   It.... Look: I don't know what you *need;* I don't know what you *want.* You have to set a price that you'd be *happy* with. It's that simple. This nonsense: "Don't lower your *quote;* Don't let them know you're hungry ..." Blah Blah Blah ... it's *true,* what can I tell you? Your objective: Get The Job. At The Price That You Want. You know and I know if they know you'll do it for ten dollars they won't spit on you to pass the *time.* So ... so ... it's *difficult.* You go too *low* ... (I know you know this ...) you're screwed; You go too high, then they sense you're *weak,* they treat you like bullshit. What is the figure you could *live* with, below which you'll blow the deal? *(Pause.)*

B.   Fifty.

A.   Is it fifty?

B.   Yes.

A.   At which you'd blow the deal?

B.   Yes.

A.   Would you take forty?

B.   No.

A.   Under no circumstances?

B.   No.

A.   All right.

B.   You think fifty is right?

A.   Yes. If you're happy with it. *(Pause.)*

B.   You don't think it's too low?
A.   No.
B.   You don't think it's too high?
A.   No. I don't. I think it's right. *(Pause.)*
B.   You do.
A.   Yes. *(Pause.)*
B.   You do.
A.   Yes. I do. *(Pause.)* Yes. *(Pause.)* I do.

Scene 2

A.   What about Tesla.
B.   Tesla.
A.   A.C. Current. A polish guy, something. Comes there, Edison tries to buy him out.
B.   What was this?
A.   Turn-of-the-Century. I don't know, 1910. Tesla. A *greater* genius, many ways, than Edison. Gets off the boat, no papers, no *nothing. Broke.*
B.   Did you need papers then?
A.   I don't know. I'm sure it helped. First thing off the boat, then he goes to Edison ... that afternoon he's working for him.... *Many* things ... *Westinghouse* ... many kinds of generators.... *Later,* A.C. current. All right? There's a lot of showmanship, this time, in electricity. Picture this: A *huge* guy. Not huge. Large. Six-four. Walks on stage, *huge* rubber soles this thick. "I'm going to run ten thousand volts through me ..." Little girl from the audience. "Come up here." They stand her on a chair, they *juice* her, all the *hair* goes on end. *(Long pause.)* All her *hair* goes on end. Many things.... You hold a coin, it's magnetized. Edison tries to buy him out. Forget it. Edison goes, tries to invent the one thing that proves the thing is dangerous. A.C., they'll take it off the ...
B.   ... what...?
A.   They'll take it off, to dis ...
B.   To ...
A.   ... to ...

B.   ... to *discredit* the ...

A.   Yes. What does Edison *invent*?

B.   What?

A.   The electric chair. He's going to show the guy up, his machine is dangerous. So, the *electric* chair.... The first guy that they juice, four hours, he's going like this *(Demonstrates.)* four hours. They've got the voltage set too low ... the *wattage* too low. *(Pause.)*

B.   "Edison the Man."

A.   Screw that. Listen to this: *meanwhile* he's living high off the hog, the Waldorf Astoria. One of the Five Hundred, the Four Hundred, what do you call it.... He goes out West. This is in Nineteen-*Ten* ... some thing, he's constructing huge towers ... millions of volts of electricity ... I don't know ... he's engendering *storms* ... he's creating *storms (Pause.)* all kinds of ... the F.B.I. is on him.

B.   Why?

A.   ... he *dies* ... before he *dies* — listen to this: he's sitting taking pictures of his ... like this: *(Demonstrates.)* of his *head* ... he's taking pictures of his *thoughts.* He dies, they go in and wipe all his plates. *(Pause.)* He's taking pictures of his *thoughts.* Seventy years old. Sitting in the Waldorf, all around, F.B.I. Agents *watching* him. Waiting for him to die. Watching him through *binoculars. (Pause.)* That sort of thing. *(Pause.)*

B.   This guy was Hu*ngari*an?

A.   I think so. Yes.

B.   What, are there *books* on him?

A.   Exerpts from books *(Pause.)* or an, an *adventure,* an *epic* ... Something that ... something that would force me to *re-educate* myself. In some way. *Research* ... difficult *locations* ... a difficult *period* ... *(Pause.) Business (Pause.) Adventure* ... *(Pause.)*

B.   A biography.

A.   Why not? *(Pause.) Anything. (Pause.)* Science ... *(Pause.)* or a *musical* ... *(Pause.) Anything* ... why not?

B.   An epic.

A.   Yes.

B.   Where?

A.   Anywhere.

B. The West.

A. No.

B. The *Northwest*. Explorers.

A. Yes. De La Salle.

B. Who was he?

A. He discovered Chicago.

B. Who was he?

A. A French Duke, something. They sent him away. His father sends him away, "Get out of here ..."

B. ... uh huh ...

A. The New *World* ...

B. ... Mmm ...

A. He goes across Lake *Michigan*, he thinks he's found the route to *India*. He lands at *Chicago*, he calls it "China." He wires back "I've found the route to the *Indies*."

B. Was this the guy down South?

A. No. I don't think so. Who?

B. I don't know. Down South.

A. No. No. I don't think so. Lots of things ... Indian *women* ...

B. Uh huh ...

A. *Indians* ...

B. Uh huh ...

A. A *lunatic* guy ...

B. Uh huh ...

A. Mucked-up guys. That's what I'm saying.

B. *Dreamers.*

A. Yes. That's what I'm *saying*. That's what I'm saying.

Scene 3

B. She keeps giving these little burps, you don't know what she's doing, like these little squeaks. She's gross. We love her, though.

A. Why?

B. Because she loves *him*.

A. Why does she love him?

B.   She's his wife.

A.   Why do *we* love him?

B.   Because he's like *us* ...

A.   In what way?

B.   He's a loser.

A.   ... mmm ...

B.   But ... he's a *loser* ... but, he's not a loser *inside*.

A.   Why? 'Cause he can "smile?"

B.   No. He can't smile.

A.   Why not?

B.   He's ... he's not "hurt" ... he's *(Pause.)* He's not "bewildered" ...

A.   What is he?

B.   He's ...

A.   Is he "charming?"

B.   No. *Yes.* In a *way.* He's "charming" ... he's not charming to *himself.*

A.   Uh huh.

B.   He's ...

A.   He's *everyman.*

B.   Yes. He's everyman. He's *all* of us. He's all of us. He's the kind ... he's the kind of guy, you know, he's ...

A.   What's the story?

B.   *Jerry,* the guy ... *(Pause.)*

A.   Yes? *(Pause.)*

B.   A *life.* A *marriage* ... *(Pause.)*

A.   But what's the story?

B.   Well. He's lost his job ...

A.   ... uh huh ...

B.   He's lost his job, and *Brenda* ... Brenda ... she's the kind of girl ... while he's out of work, *one* day she might, well, she's kooky, you know, but we love her. One d ...

A.   Why?

B.   ... well ... *(Pause.)* One, one day she ... she brings home a book: "Living on a ..." I'm sorry ... *he* brings the ... this is funny ... *he* brings the book home, they have a fight about what the *book* cost. You see? He can't do anything right. It's a simple, funny ...

A. And what does the guy *do?* I mean, what does he *do?*

B. He's a flight instructor.

A. Uh huh.

B. And he's out of work, because his *boss* — all right? —

A. ... uh huh ...

B. ... his boss ...

A. ... his boss owns the airplane ...

B. Yes. His boss is a compulsive gambler ...

A. He keeps ... he loses the planes?

B. He's lost the ... Brenda's terrified of flying.

A. ... uh huh ...

B. ... Jo-Jo's lost ... they're more like *brothers,* really ... Jo-Jo's *older* ... he's from a different background.

A. ... mmm ...

B. ... now *he's* a funny guy. He:

A. Jo-Jo lost the planes.

B. Yes.

A. To Organized Crime?

B. No.

A. Mmm.

B. And, see, but he's not *bad* ... he's "unlucky" ...

A. Uh huh ...

B. So ...

A. ... so different times he gets lucky, he wins his *planes* back.

B. *Sure.*

A. Jerry's 'bout to go out on a new job he just got, the guy says "Come back to work," before Jerry gets there the guy lost the planes again.

B. Yes.

A. Good. And Brenda, "Blah blah *blah,* learn a *trade* don't hang your life on this bozo ..."

B. ... he loves flying.

A. ... *so* on ...

B. Mmm. They were in Vietnam together.

A. Uh huh.

B. There's this *other* flight instructor.

A. ... also out-of-work...?

B.   A broad. Yes.

A.   A broad.

B.   Yes. But what a broad. A ... with a *difference (Pause.)* a golden girl. A golden girl ... a *sunset* girl ...

A.   Uh huh ...

B.   But funny ...

A.   Umm.

B.   She ...

Scene 4

A.   So how's things? *(Pause.)*

B.   What do you mean? *(Pause.)*

A.   How's *things*?

B.   What do you mean?

A.   I mean how are things.

B.   How do you *think* they are? They're *fine*. What do you mean?

A.   I, uh ..

B.   I mean, what do you mean? What do you want me to say?

A.   What are you talking about?

B.   What am I *talking* about? What am I *talking* about ... what gives you the right ... what am I *talking* about, what do you want me to do, jump through a *hoop*?

A.   What are you talking about?

B.   Where have you been? Where have you been the last ... where have you been? *(Pause.)*

A.   In the Islands.

B.   You've ... you've been in the Islands. Fine. Fine. When did you get back? You're back now. When did you get back?

A.   When did I get back?

B.   Yes.

A.   I got back yesterday.

B.   You did.

A.   Yes.

B.   You got back yesterday.

A.   I got back last night.

B.   You got back last night. And you didn't ... you got back last ... and don't know what happened to me.

A.   No.

B.   You're telling me in the "Islands" you didn't hear, you don't know what I'm talking about?

A.   What are you talking about?

B.   You're saying that you don't know what I'm talking about, you're saying you just walked *over* here: "How are you?" "The *Weather* ..."

A.   Bob:

B.   Why? Why now? *Stand* there, you *stand* there and *tell* me that this isn't cheap *thrills* ... this isn't prurient ...

A.   ... what the hell are you talking about?

B.   What am I *talking* about ... what am I *talking* about? Screw you.

A.   What are you talking about, for God ...

B.   You ... you ... you ... you ... you're a cheap.... You're a damn piece of *scum,* Sid. You know that? You're *cheap.* You really are. You always were. You always said you were my friend, screw you ...

A.   Bob ...

B.   You ... you ...

A.   Bob, *please,* I've, I've been ... what the hell are you *talking* about, for God's sake?

B.   You don't know what I'm talking about?

A.   That's what I'm ...

B.   Swear it. *(Pause.)* Swear it. *(Pause.)* On your children's life. *(Pause.)* Do it. 'Cause it's been a hard ... swear it. Sid. 'Cause it's been a hard ... it's been a hard week. You don't ... swear you don't know what I'm talking about, because everybody in this town is pissing in my mouth this week what happened; people that I haven't seen in years crossing the street to accidentally say hello, so they can laugh at me. So they can snicker at me. So you'll have to excuse me ... you'll have to pardon me, you understand...?

A.   I don't know what you're talking about, Bobby.

B.   Swear it.

A. I swear.

B. Swear it on your children's life.

A. I swear it on my children's life.

B.   Then may you rot in hell, because I talked to Jo, she told me she saw you at Jimmy's last night and she told you the whole thing.

Scene 5

A.   Words of power. Words with power. Words with power. These words have no power in them. They have no power to move. Where is the strength in them? No. He's on the top of the world. There is the fable he reads to his kids. The Blah Blah Blah, the Prince, the King, "You shall be evermore, unless you *say* at anytime I am The King" (the Prince, whatever that he is). He reads it to his kids. One day on television. "Of your" ... "tell us of," to, eh? Compare himself. "What is your ..." eh? "Opinions of...?" He, who says why? For this, for that ... compare his *fellows*. And, of course, he's thought about it ... "I think, certainly, I am the ..." he says he's the best. He says it. *Instantly* ... not instantly ... slowly ... not with any great amount of time ... he is transformed. Here's how it happens: In the newspapers there is a furor: "So and so, the famous, speaking of himself on national ... he said he was the best ..." Now, this becomes a joke. How he — if the fable concerns *humility* ... he's *revealed* himself. He's spoken out. You say: "A Secret Name." "What power is in it?" There's power for a reason. What is it? In this case, self-pro ... or we have to say, "humility," if that's to put his place between the Apes and Angels. At the school where he, the enrollment drops off — they, you know, the kids don't like to be seen — they don't like to be thought ri — he's made himself ridiculous. Now no one will do his work. The work that he *had* done they look back on, "How could I have admired this ..." Because he's *violated* them. The utmost censure they can ... they find him ... it goes *beyond* ... they have, you know, *truly* ... they have *ostracized* him.... *Right* out.... They

78

find him ridiculous. "Who is this bozo?" So on, his wife leaves him ... also: Also: (speaking of humility) what has he done? He's tempted God. "That's fine for *you*, but there's these *others*, we're here, *too*, around the campfire ..." So, in some way, it's *right* — He *should* be ... as an action of the group, they're, they *must*, or else, they're, in a true sense, they're unprotected. His wife leaves him. Everything is gone. The worst, of course, is he knows why — although he'd like to — it was his own doing. Down and out, he calls on God. "I'm sorry." "Tough tit," actually. He, all he had to do was keep the charm. He couldn't do it. That's what happened to him. And that's why I say you should pay close attention to the stories that you read your kid.

A LIFE WITH
NO JOY IN IT

A LIFE WITH NO JOY IN IT

A — A man in his mid-fifties.

B — A woman of around thirty.

A.   A teaspoon.

B.   Is that a teaspoon?

A.   Yes. It is.

B.   A teaspoon. As if you would say a "*Teas*-poon," but for tea.

A.   Yes.

B.   With hinged ... with *hinges.*

A.   Yes.

B.   With *jaws.*

A.   That open. Yes.

B.   And is that where that phrase comes from?

A.   Yes. Must be.

B.   You think so? Yes?

A.   ... mmm.

B.   That our modern *teas-poon* comes.

A.   Yes.

B.   From a "spoon." Of course, that must be the thing. Then we do we resist it?

A.   You said "New York?"

B.   Like the one we had there.

A.   You remembered it there?

B.   ... we had one ...

A.   Yes. *(Pause.)* You remembered it. *(Pause.)*

B.   Is it odd that I remembered it?

A.   It was so long ago.

B.   No.

A.   "Not to *you*...?"

B.   No. Not to me. No. What?

A.   It was so long ago. Darling. You were so young.

B.   I, wasn't that you.

A.   That's what you're saying. No.

B.   I wasn't that young.

A.   Yes. I see that. *(Pause.)* I see that. *(Pause.)* Yes. *(Pause.)* Aha. Do you know. As you live, more and more, as you step back from it, you can see more of, if not the *order,* at least, of the *pattern.* Do you think? But perhaps it just means you are removed from it. *(Pause.)* *Removed* from it. *(Pause.)* And, you see, then, through.... When something shines through ... when you are *done* with it — it breaks on you, you see. You are done with it. You've put it to rest, and you see the sadness less. And you feel that's true. You feel ... you've finally achieved "philosophy." Which you sought. And which eluded you. And when you see that it has come upon you, you can feel no *honor* in it. And it signifies no merit, but that you have *lived.* Until a certain time. Where you no longer *desire* those things you desired. And, calling this "philosophy," you question if "philosophy," you see, if it *exists.* Or, or, that it *exists,* but that those who *expounded* it, must finally have been other than the tired, and the sinful, and the confused thing that *I* am. And they must have been *better* than me, who have reached this state of non-desire through dull sloth, and you cannot even say it's *persistence.* No, you say, those men were not as sinful as *I* am. They were *good,* and reasoned *purely.* And, further, that that was not the case. They were as sinful as oneself, and spoke from nothing other than fatigue, and resignation. And this thought destroys philosophy, and what was peace is now only fatigue. The joys are less, the pain is less. But the joys ... but the pain, you see, has been lessened, but the *joys* have been *obliterated.* "Well," you say ... *(Pause.)*

B.   What are you telling me?

A.   I'm telling you I'm sorry.

B.   Would you like your tea?

A.   Yes. Thank you. *(Pause.)* The lassitude. It caused. It drained me.

B.   The tea did?

A.   The tea. It enervated me. The afternoons. That we would spend together. I'd try to refrain from drinking it. I wouldn't try to refrain. I would *wish* to refrain. I would not wish to refrain, if I'd wished to do so I would have done so. I would say, "why do you drink it?" And I would drink it. I sat outside. At this Teak Set. Of constructed furniture. I suppose much of Modern Life is in aid of that sort of fashion meant to emphasize stability; as, in an earlier time, we saw emphasis upon the evanescent. *(Pause.)* Didn't we?

B.   I don't know.

A.   In the Postmodern?

B.   I don't know.

A.   In the ... in *Deconstructivism?* In that "art" which was no way superior to a description given of it? In that which was not art. It was not decor, it was not *politics* ... what was it? It was assault. It was, if we may use this word, *anger.* We could say "obscenity," but it was not obscene, it was vile. It was vicious — for all that we wrote against it. *(Pause.)* Not that it mattered. *(Pause.)* It *didn't* matter. What do we *not* ascribe purpose to...?

B.   I don't ...

A.   ... and say:

B.   ... I don't understand.

A.   "I thought that I was *attacked* ... and *hated* ... and I was *humiliated* by that art, that *art,* that which to my mind was not art, but *hurtfulness* and pain seeking a victim. And I was *angered* by it. I see now there was a higher purpose! And that very hurt I felt ..." Do you see?

B.   No.

A.   "... in your treatment of me. When I was so wretched. And I was mistreated. When I was *bereft* ... when I reached out for comfort, and was hurt. And you rejected me. And subjugated me. And trained me to self-hate and to revulsion. And to hatred of the very thoughts I had. And what could I say, being helpless? But to wish to kill, or to wish to die, or to say...'Ah, Ah. I *see!* I *see* now, that you, who were so powerful.' You who had power over me. That you were *right!!!*" Do you see? "Modern Art." "I *was,* I *did,* I *was,* I *did mis un der stand you.*" I see now ..."

B.   ... that there was meaning?

A.   Yes.

B.   ... when there was not.

A.   *As* there was not. There was none in it.

B.   I remember watching the rain. From the window. And I said, "I cannot tell if it was raining." And you said, "Two ways are to watch for the *cars* ..."

A.   ... yes.

B.   "... and watch their windshield wipers. Or ..." And gave me to feel that this was the more elegant ...

A.   ... as it was ...

B.   What was it...?

A.   The drops in the puddles.

B.   And felt ... the drops in the puddles — not only ...

A.   ... as it was.

B.   ... it was more *elegant,* but ...

A.   Yes.

B.   Which, perhaps, you meant, if you meant it ...

A.   ... if I did ...

B.   ... as the *meaning* of elegance. "Here is a model whereby you may choose the better of two choices. As they come to you: Which is more *basic?* Which of the two is more *natural?* Which is the less *adorned?* Which of the two — perhaps this is most important — could have been employed before the present day — in the *woods* — in the eighteenth *century?* Which, then, avoids the hatedly contrived and the mechanical?" If we could see that, we could live in a world which does not exist, but which *perhaps* exists. That world, that basic world below this. *Is this what you meant?* The image of a man I took with me? As per your investiture with all wisdom. Which we give to those we adore. Do we? Good or bad? Is that what you meant? Yes. That I thought that of you. And I remember the tea spoon. And the remember the evenings, and the rain, which I could not say had stopped falling. I remember evenings. And how many times I said, "don't go," and how guilty you felt. And how I loved you. And how I missed you. And how much I love you. And your worry about

86

modern art. And how you say it all is at an end, and wrack your brain for any evidence that you are wrong, and find none, and look beyond, for any meaning to this end, and resist calling it philosophy, and come to say it is philosophy, but that you are unworthy to enjoy it as such, being worthless, as you think you are, and come to it only through ignorance and pain. I hate this weather. It ain't going to change. *(Pause.)* When are you going back?

A.   I'm going back soon.

B.   I took the little one to school. I didn't take her to school, I *went* to school. I saw it.

A.   How is it?

B.   It's fine.

A.   She going to like it?

B.   Yes.

A.   What did you think of Sarah?

B.   She was absolutely false.

A.   Did you think so?

B.   Yes. I know you did, too.

A.   I never liked her.

B.   No?

A.   *(Pause.) People* ...

B.   No. I never liked her, either ...

A.   Why?

B.   Because she is *false. (Pause.)*

A.   *People* ...

B.   ... yes?

A.   ... and perhaps you have not seen this. Probably you have not seen enough of them, and why should you have?... tend to behave terribly falsely at funerals. I don't know ...

B.   ... yes?

A.   ... those that ... those that. Those that come "up" to one ...

B.   ... I think express themselves quite well.

A.   Yes. I do, too.

B.   And laudably, in fact.

A.   Yes. I do, too. I ... *truthfully* and with *restraint,* and most importantly ...

B.   ... yes?

A.   Neither *overcome,* nor ... that is, overcome *by,* nor, nor ... *overcoming* their emotions. Those who *speak,* however ...

B.   Yes. They're *false.* You ...

A.   ... and we may make allowance for the fact they do not speak in public.

B.   No.

A.   ... with regularity.

B.   No. I don't like their *disclaimer.* I don't like their tone ... "I hardly *knew* her ..."

A.   ... yes.

B.   ... or "I hadn't seen her in twenty years, but still ..."

A.   Mmm.

B.   Or, "two children never were closer." Or, "you must excuse me ..." Did you see how many began, "you must ..."

A.   ... yes.

B.   Well. They began with an imperative.

A.   It's an imperative, yes.

B.   Why? *(Pause.)* In speaking of the dead?

A.   ... no one ever likes the things the clergyman says ...

B.   ... I'm sure that that's true. But the "bright," and the "sunny," and the stupid Women's Poetry, and "like a butterfly," and "The Free Spirit Flying ..." and her "ever-present cup of tea ..." Her "endless cups of tea." Well. She Drank *Tea.* She "did" many things. "I never knew *you,* but, in knowing *her,* I feel I know you." You *don't* know me. You don't know me and you didn't know *her, fool.* Who do you think you are? I *suffered* with her for years, and spent my waking and sleeping hours trying to understand. And you tell me you "knew" her, and she was "a walk in a night's garden"...? And the *other* one ... what was her name? What are *you* doing there...? And "her love of jazz." "The world was one improvisation to her." Well. How about that? "Just one long melody of thoughts and people. Sand in your Summer Shoes and the crinkle of logs in the wood stove ..." Thank you. *(Pause.) Thank* you. And endless cups of tea. And how we loved you all. The *three* of you. And we *know* that she is at peace. Well. If she is at peace, then I mistake her. *(Pause.).* As a reward, or as a commutation. Then I didn't know her at all. But I *did* know her. They didn't know her. I knew her. Did you know her, too? What shall I say? You're going when? Soon. Yes. A Life of Work.

A.   I ... *(Pause.)*

B.   I'm sorry. *(Pause.)* Aren't those the sweetest words? *(Pause.)*

A.   But what can bring it back?

B.   No, indeed.

A.   And we are not those people.

B.   Which?

A.   The false people.

B.   No.

A.   We are ...

B.   ... no ...

A.   We are you and me.

B.   ... isn't that so...?

A.   ... who made a fire in the woods. I understand. I used to think, "not enough. Not enough." It was not the time. *(Pause.)* It was the trauma. *(Pause.)* Because the time ... the time would have passed — in *any* case.

JOSEPH DINTENFASS

JOSEPH DINTENFASS

Joseph — a man in his fifties.
Claire — a woman in her twenties.
The living room of his house in the country.

JOSEPH.   There are people who have a horror of existence. I don't know. I may be one of them. What do you *think?* *(Pause.)*
CLAIRE.   We saw a deer on our way up.
JOSEPH.   *Did* you.
CLAIRE.   Near Springfield.
JOSEPH.   By the road?
CLAIRE.   No. It was in the road. At dusk. We almost hit it.
JOSEPH.   Mm. Mmm. *(Pause.)*
CLAIRE.   I think that it was large. It's difficult to say. We came over a *rise* ...
JOSEPH.   A stag?
CLAIRE.   Yes.
JOSEPH.   Did he have horns?
CLAIRE.   Yes. He did.
JOSEPH.   You know, we have them here.
CLAIRE.   Yes. Michael told me that you did.
JOSEPH.   *You'll* see them ... I don't know. I used to see them all the time.
CLAIRE.   Do you put things out for them?
JOSEPH.   Did I put things out for them. No. They. Live ... *(Pause.)* They're what is called "*edge* feeders." They live on the ... or "*margin* feeders ..." They live on the margin of the woods.
CLAIRE.   Why do ...
JOSEPH.   Why? *(Pause.)*
CLAIRE.   Why do they call them that?

JOSEPH.   They live on new growth. *(Pause.)* Do you understand?

CLAIRE.   On the ...

JOSEPH.   Yes.

CLAIRE.   On the growth of the trees that takes place on the ...

JOSEPH.   Yes.

CLAIRE.   *(Pause.)* Mm.

JOSEPH.   The trees and bushes. And I shouldn't talk that way, because I don't know anything about them either. Just that phrase. But I was going to say.... *(Pause.)* There's something to do with salt. They need it for *digestion* ... or for ... I don't know. I think we used to put it out. Years ago.

CLAIRE.   A block.

JOSEPH.   Yes.

CLAIRE.   A "salt lick."

JOSEPH.   Yes.

CLAIRE.   How heavy were the blocks?

JOSEPH.   I think they weren't too heavy. I think they were *large*. Like this ... not too ... I was going to say perhaps "not tightly *packed*," but I'm sure they would *have* to be. When you think of a bag of salt. Perhaps I never moved them.

CLAIRE.   But who moved them, then?

JOSEPH.   Well, I must have, that's right. You try ... you'll do this, too. I know. Perhaps you won't ... there seems to be a destiny that *leads* you — to those things you can and *cannot* do ... as much as I ... for example ... *(Pause.)* would want to be a part of this *community* ... and had planned for years to *be* so ....to *rise* early. *(Pause.)* To ... *(Pause.)* To have *animals* ... you look down the road and say "In ten years I could be an accomplished *farmer*" ... or better than that: I could use skills they *don't* possess, and reclaim *expertise* ... *(Pause.)* they had lost ... weaving, or something. Blacksmithing ... because I have the *time* ... and ... *(A long pause.)*

CLAIRE.   I ...

JOSEPH.   And, and, and intellectual ... *(Pause.)* *Curiosity*. You never *do*, however. Some people do. Friends of mine. Up here. Many of them. I remained, in most ways — and I, and

I'm sure the very fact of my finding the area continually picturesque through all this time supported me in this — I remained an outsider. And who carried the thing *out,* after all these years ... *(Pause.)* Is a.... *(Pause.)* Because it was a *fantasy,* you see. I was an *outsider.* Hm. *(Pause.)* It's not such a bad thing to be.

CLAIRE. No.

JOSEPH. You don't think so.

CLAIRE. No.

JOSEPH. Have you felt it?

CLAIRE. Yes. I think I have.

JOSEPH. Then you know what I mean. It's easy to become fixated. I don't know. As I grow older my mind seems to go more ... not like childhood, but like adolescence.

CLAIRE. How do you mean?

JOSEPH. *Thinking* about things.

CLAIRE. What things?

JOSEPH. What things?

CLAIRE. Yes.

JOSEPH. Anything. A lock. I bought a lock when I was in the city. All the way home I was thinking when I get home I would snap the lock on. Eh? When I walked in the door. That was the first thing I would do. I *knew* that was what I would do. I knew that was what I would do. *(Pause.)* Although it was ... I could have *waited.* And I know that it was *useless....* No, I won't say useless ... it wasn't *important. (Pause.)* There was nothing important about it. And I thought of it all the way down and all the way back. And walking in I said to myself, "Don't do it," and I did it anyway. And I knew that I would. I used to do my mail standing up when we'd been away. You know, when it had been piling up. In my overcoat ...

CLAIRE. ... where?

JOSEPH. Where did I do it?

CLAIRE. Yes.

JOSEPH. At the kitchen table.

CLAIRE. Is that where it was?

JOSEPH. What? The mail. They put it there. Yes. I stood

there ... *(Pause.)*

CLAIRE. Did you enjoy it?

JOSEPH. Yes. I did. *(Pause.)*

CLAIRE. What was the lock for?

JOSEPH. A cabinet.

CLAIRE. We all have things like that.

JOSEPH. You think so? Yes. I know we do. *(Pause.)*

CLAIRE. We all do.

JOSEPH. What are yours?

CLAIRE. Appointments.

JOSEPH. Mmm. *(Pause.)*

CLAIRE. Many things.

JOSEPH. *Collections.* *(Pause.)* My ... *(Pause.)* Collections ... *(Pause.)* Antiques ... you know, *habit.* *(Pause.)* Years ... *(Pause.)* Years I would say, "Why do I *lust* after this thing...?"

CLAIRE. What thing?

JOSEPH. Whatever it was. Something for a *collection* of mine ... *figures* ... any ... I would say "It's only made of *stone*" ... or *wood.* And why was I driven to ... *(Pause.)* To *own* it, or to *have* it, and what did it mean if I did *not*? And it meant *nothing*, of course. And I couldn't ... *(Pause.)* I'd go to a show or a dealer *(Pause.)* Or I would *pay* too much. Or ... *(Pause.)* Well. I don't have to tell you what I'm talking about ... and, but ... *(Pause.)* And I was younger then.... But ... what did it mean? If I'd *had* it — if I *hadn't* had it ... when I'd seen the *folly* of it. And I did it *anyway.*

CLAIRE. And what was it in adolescence?

JOSEPH. I don't understand what you mean.

CLAIRE. What ...

JOSEPH. What was I *driven* to?

CLAIRE. Yes.

JOSEPH. I suppose that it was no more. I don't know. It must have been. You know, it's funny. Because it wasn't just then either, of course. I think of it, and it's been, I suppose that that's the ... it's been *constant.* It *has* been constant. *(Pause.)* Things you order through the *mail* ... *(Pause.)*

CLAIRE. Things you *say.* *(Pause.)*

JOSEPH. *Yes.*

CLAIRE. Isn't it ...

JOSEPH. Yes.

CLAIRE. The things we say. Many times. I don't know where they come from. Ideas. *(Pause.)* I don't know where they come from. *(Pause.)* Thoughts. *(Pause.)* Images that we have. *(Pause.)* Or also what they *do.*

JOSEPH. What do you mean?

CLAIRE. When we *say* them. *(Pause.)* When we *say* them and the effect that they have. I think in many ways that it's mysterious. If you think ... if you think, if you think about the fact an impulse comes and we — it comes into our head from somewhere and we act on it, however we do, and. *(Pause.)* In some way it affects those around us. *(Pause.)* And then ... *(Pause.)* And then it is in *them.* Beyond them — in their *mind.* *(Pause.)* In their understanding of the way things are. Or something they have *seen.* *(Pause.)* Colors people wear. *(Pause.)* Thoughts. *(Pause.)* Thoughts we have. Impressions when we're going to *meet* someone. That's an example. If we've heard about them. *(Pause.)* And famous people certainly. And *anyone* ... who has the power to awaken interest. *(Pause.)* I think that that's the important thing. *(Pause.)* And do you know one thing that I like? Trademarks.

JOSEPH. I do, too.

CLAIRE. Especially old ones.

JOSEPH. I do, too.

CLAIRE. And, well, I'll tell you something else: I know you do.

JOSEPH. How do you know that?

CLAIRE. Michael told me. And when he did I said, "I like that, *too.*" Because I'd never said it to myself. What it was. Or: *(Pause.)* I'd never *phrased* to myself my appreciation of them; but they made me feel *calm,* and when I *thought* of them — when he told me — I saw what it was was they made me feel things would continue. And I *liked* them. And I said, "*That* is the kind of person that I am." What do you think about that? *(Pause.)*

JOSEPH. I think it's important.

CLAIRE. You do. Why?

JOSEPH.   Because it's important to *you*. *(Pause.)*
CLAIRE.   And I think there are people you can *speak* to. And I think there are those that you can't. And ... *(Pause.)* And I'll tell you what: there are so many thing we don't *know,* we don't know what they *are. Fatigue* ... or *sleep. (Pause.)* Or *numbers* ... for example we ... mm ... we ... *(Long pause.)*
JOSEPH.   You must be tired.
CLAIRE.   I don't know. I think ...
JOSEPH.   Are you tired? You must be tired.
CLAIRE.   I wasn't driving. I'll tell you what a *bad* thing is: when you arrive somewhere and you're tired, but you cannot sleep. And the best thing is when you go to sleep. *(Pause.)*
JOSEPH.   Do you want to go up?
CLAIRE.   No.
JOSEPH.   Are you sure? Because if you want to you should.
CLAIRE.   I'm positive.
JOSEPH.   *He's* asleep.
CLAIRE.   Yes. He's *been* here before.
JOSEPH.   You'll ...
CLAIRE.   Perhaps. And, you know, maybe and may be not. It's not important. *(Pause.)* You can't fulfill desire in any case.
JOSEPH.   What do ...
CLAIRE.   It's not important. I stayed in a hotel once with linen sheets. When I laid *down* I said "These are the finest sheets ... they're *coarse.*" I didn't know what they *were* ... *(Pause.)* When you learn a *word,* you don't know what it *is* ... you have a *meaning* for it, or the lyrics of a song, when you don't hear it, on the *radio,* say when you're in a car, and you can't hear the lyrics, or you *think* you do, and. They make perfect sense. *Later:* when you learn the *true* words, then they're not as *good,* and I thought *(Pause.)* "These sheets are *starched. That's* all ... they're *starched.* I'll rub my face in them and I'll be *scratched. Later,* you know, *later* he said "Linen sheets." But then they never felt the same. "Oh, linen feels like starch." And so we insulate ourselves about a new experience; and when I used to learn a word I said it was a treasure. *Later* I said "A new word for something which *exists.*" Sex was like that, of course, and *learning* ... I'm sure that there are

98

experiences beyond me — but I don't know what they *are,* and I haven't *found* them. Now I'm so protected. I know I must seek them out. I know now that what I must change is *myself.* And the ... oh, this is so *lonely* though, don't you think? I know if I would change myself then the world might open. But it isn't the same. *Is* it?

JOSEPH.   No.

CLAIRE.   No. Not at all. And on the other hand perhaps there are degrees of wisdom. And, again, it isn't the same.

JOSEPH.   And, again, it isn't the same. *(Pause.)*

CLAIRE.   No. *(Pause.)* ... except when I say *wisdom,* then, perhaps it is. Isn't it? *(Pause.)* If what it is is wisdom. *(Pause.)*

JOSEPH.   Yes.

CLAIRE.   I know that. *(Pause.)* But love is not.

JOSEPH.   No.

CLAIRE.   The love of a child, perhaps?

JOSEPH.   Perhaps.

CLAIRE.   The love *for* a child.

JOSEPH.   Is that what you meant?

CLAIRE.   Yes.

JOSEPH.   Then perhaps it is.

CLAIRE.   *Is* it?

JOSEPH.   Yes.

CLAIRE.   But it's not the same.

JOSEPH.   No.

CLAIRE.   *Is* it?

JOSEPH.   No.

CLAIRE.   And you know that.

JOSEPH.   Yes.

CLAIRE.   Yes. But it's worthwhile.

JOSEPH.   Yes.

CLAIRE.   Yes. I know it is.

JOSEPH.   It's more than worthwhile. *(Pause.)*

CLAIRE.   But it's *shared. Isn't* it...?

JOSEPH.   For men, perhaps. For women, I don't know. I don't *think* so.

CLAIRE.   You don't think that it's shared?

JOSEPH.   No. *(Pause.)*

CLAIRE. I think I'm too much like a man. (Pa*use.*) We all wish that we could surrender. *Don't* we?

JOSEPH. At some ... at ... in some ways we do. At some level. The ...

CLAIRE. We see both sides. Don't we?

JOSEPH. I think we do.

CLAIRE. We always ... (*Pause.*) And that's the trouble. (*Pause.*) That's ...

JOSEPH. Tomorrow ...

CLAIRE. Are you going to bed? Oh. Do, I'm sorry, do you, am I ... I'm keeping you ...

JOSEPH. ... no.

CLAIRE. Yes. I see that I am. I'm sorry. (*She gets up.*)

JOSEPH. No, don't ...

CLAIRE. I'm sorry. I'm being a bad guest. I'll.... No, I'll ... (*Pause.*) Goodnight. Do you mind...? (*She goes to him and kisses him.*)

JOSEPH. I didn't mean.

CLAIRE. (*Simultaneously with above.*) Was that...?

JOSEPH. I'm sorry?

CLAIRE. What? I'm sorry. What did you say? I think that I'm tired. You know, if I could have ... I think I'm overtired ... not overtired, I'm just ... (*She pours a whiskey.*) Do you mind?

JOSEPH. Not at all.

CLAIRE. Would you like some?

JOSEPH. Thank you. (*She pours a glass for him.*)

CLAIRE. Oh! It's been a long day.

JOSEPH. And did he pick you up at ...

CLAIRE. Yes. He picked me up at work. And I'll tell you what I think we did wrong. We ate before the drive. And I think ... I always thought you shouldn't eat when you're traveling. Don't you think? You know why? Because you need to *float*. Really. My new theory is everything is literal.

JOSEPH. I think that's very true.

CLAIRE. Do you? I do, too. I think that's a good feeling, to know that nothing is hidden. Also traveling you shouldn't bring along the things behind. To *bring* them, literally ...

(Pause.) To be *digesting* them while ...

JOSEPH.   Yes.

CLAIRE.   While you're traveling. To be un*cum*bered I think I'm getting tired. What were we saying?

JOSEPH.   Do you ... do you...?

CLAIRE.   I *am* getting tired. Do I what?

JOSEPH.   Do you have everything you need?

CLAIRE.   *Upstairs. Upstairs,* you mean? Do I have everything I need?

JOSEPH.   Yes.

CLAIRE.   Yes. And I wanted to tell you your house is lovely.

JOSEPH.   Thank you.

CLAIRE.   It is ... *(Pause.)* And ... *(Pause.)* Well, I'll *say* it, and the *amenities* that you've ... you know. I always ... what I valued was a *style.* A sense of style. A *style.* Even when I had money. If I had it for a while. Or I was with a man who did. I never, and I seldom with them — I don't think I ever — other people's houses. *(Pause.)* Or their *apartments* ... *(Pause.)* I think that dress is easier ... would be *complete;* and when I *went* there I would feel *peaceful. (Pause.)* Mine never was.*(Pause.)* I would spend money on it, and still ...

JOSEPH.   It expressed you.

CLAIRE.   ... and when someone was especially peaceful *(Pause.)* It may be an illusion. I don't know. I know that much of it is not. *(Pause.)* Here. *(Pause.)* I don't think Michael sees it, even. What is it? The feminine touch. I don't know.

JOSEPH.   He doesn't see it?

CLAIRE.   No.

JOSEPH.   And what is it he doesn't see?

CLAIRE.   Your ... maybe he does ... maybe I'm wrong. *Calm.* Your house ... he, he, he, he's not *sensitive.* You know that. He's *expressive.* That's why ... that's what *I* am.

JOSEPH.   What is that?

CLAIRE.   Sensitive. I don't care. It's true. That's why whenever I live, oh ... *(Sighs.)* I don't want to talk about myself. I think it's time for me to go to bed. One thing I'd like to do. If I could. I'd like to see your collection.

JOSEPH.   Which one is that?

CLAIRE.   The one you told me. In the case. There I go.
Apostrophizing everything. *That's* a bad habit. I'm such a fool.
Really I am. I am a fraud. You know, you know, I, I ... I want
you to tell me everything. That's what I want.
JOSEPH.   What is that?
CLAIRE.   Everything.
JOSEPH.   What does that mean to you?
CLAIRE.   That's, that's, you see? That's how I thought you
talked to *Michael. (Pause.)* What's wrong with *that,* though?
Everyone is curious. I *wanted* to come here. That's what I
meant. I told you that. We all have hidden, don't you think?
JOSEPH.   What?
CLAIRE.   *Motives.* None of us is pure. Perhaps I *use* people,
I don't know. There's a point you, when you feel *something* ...
you're suffering in *any* case. Don't you...? "This is the kind of
person that I am." I have these *thoughts.* I say that's all they
are is thoughts. I have them *anyway.* And there are other
people, too. I don't think everyone's that way. And there are
people that you *use,* and I'm sure that you use them, *too.* I
could be wrong. To *come* here, in that way I thought you
talked to *him,* to talk to *me* ...
JOSEPH.   ... and what was that?
CLAIRE.   To *tell* me things. I *told* you.
JOSEPH.   And to tell you what?
CLAIRE.   It doesn't matter, really. Everyone is curious. Don't
you think that? We, "What is in the cabinet?" I thought it was
prying. I don't anymore. I *do.* I wish I didn't ... I would like
to think it was our longing for *frankness.* One way to say that
is *secrets.* One way is the personal things. What goes on in
people's bedrooms. How they act when they're alone ... the
habits that they have. A frankness ... *(Pause.)* I saw one of
your workbooks with the marbled top. Where you'd ... you
know what I mean. I, I've *read* about it. Where you fill the
spots in ... I *saw* it. It's *true.* There are things we *can* do that
impress each other.
JOSEPH.   I don't find you unimpressive.
CLAIRE.   But tell me *why.* Because I've done nothing. The
things I've done ... I know the ways in which I'm evil.

Through sloth ... through ma*nip*ulativeness ...

JOSEPH.   You don't have to confess to me.

CLAIRE.   Well, there's no one ...

JOSEPH.   ... you've done ...

CLAIRE.   ... who would I confess to ...

JOSEPH.   You've ...

CLAIRE.   ... there's no one to *talk* to. There's no one I *could* confess to. So I *came* here.

JOSEPH.   I've been looking forward to meeting you.

CLAIRE.   What, because of *Michael* ... listen to this: there are many things I could confess. I feel you know them. Why shouldn't you? What does it mean? Things provoke us. Things upset us. What can anyone confess? That they're bad. It means nothing.

JOSEPH.   It means that we put ourselves in the hands of someone more powerful.

CLAIRE.   Yes. I know that.

JOSEPH.   We elect them to control us for a time. And if we're blessed, or if we're *touched* with consciousness, that consciousness is also a price that we pay. We want to lay it down. It's difficult to surrender. It feels like death. (Pause.) We all need renewal ... we ... *release* ... (Pause.) new ... (Pause.) new ... (Pause.) Things we thought.... You're absolutely right. Who can live with them? (Pause.) No one. No one can. No. That's absolutely right. We ... (Pause.)

CLAIRE.   (To herself.) Or by now it's, it's strong, and could give strength ...

JOSEPH.   Yes, of course ... (Pause.) Now ... (Pause.) Now ... (Pause.) if we could ... (Pause.) if we could ... and you feel the world pulling away from you. Because you ... I don't (Pause.) I don't mean other people. That's ... (Pause.) That's not necessarily ... but the *world:*   you (Pause.) It pulls away. Because you have been graced.

CLAIRE.   What do you...?

JOSEPH.   It seems ... if ...

CLAIRE.   If one is *diff*erent.

JOSEPH.   No. No. Not because of ... (Pause.) Because of *luck.* Because of ... not because of *talent.* (Pause.) A lovely woman,

103

for example. *(Pause.)* Something that comes by *grace.* The *(Pause.)* Days. Days when you're walking down the street — or in a *taxi* something could *(Pause.)* *fall* on you ... kill you ... We don't, we don't know what it means when we wish for something. And, of course, a reward we've always had. If we: the *burden* of a ... like a lovely, I said that, I think that it's analogous.

CLAIRE.   We don't know what a wish means?

JOSEPH.   That's ... *yes. Yes.* To what extent

CLAIRE.   ... it ...

JOSEPH.   ... it influences what occurs.

CLAIRE.   ... it influences what occurs.

JOSEPH.   Yes.

CLAIRE.   And what do you think?

JOSEPH.   I don't know. I think to a great extent.

CLAIRE.   You do?

JOSEPH.   Yes. *(Pause.)* Don't you?

CLAIRE.   And what do *you* wish for...?

JOSEPH.   I, um ... for ... I scratched the table. We'd paid too much for it ... and ... a floor we painted. In this house.... We ... we try to acquire a history. And by, by, by *accident* we, it seems that we *do.* And that ... and that ... you ...

CLAIRE.   What do you wish for?

JOSEPH.   What do I *truly*? A society, for a secret society of wise men who one day would summon me and make me one of their number. For a ...

CLAIRE.   What do you wish for *now...?* What do you wish for tonight?

JOSEPH.   Ah. *(Pause.)* Well, that makes my answer somewhat ri ... you must excuse me. *(Pause.)* What could I give you?

CLAIRE.   ... what have I...?

JOSEPH.   ... or anyone? Or anyone give me? Who was he. Finally?... Ah. Yes. I knew him. I.... One man says something. Others find it picturesque. It's just a story. *(Pause.)* One person tells it, and another hears. Do you understand?

CLAIRE.   I don't know. *(Pause.)* I don't *know* if I do. How can I ...

JOSEPH.   *(Simultaneous with "I.")* They were just *"stories."* They were just things people *said*. There was no, there was no *magic* in them. I cannot.... You say I *can,* but ... but.... Look: papers in, a mark in books, you said, a paper. Who left it? Someone. Do I know who? Someone had been there bef ... our *lives* — spent, in an, if you go that way. An effort to ... what did the paper *mean?* People deciphered it, and it meant *nothing.* *(Pause.)* What *could* it mean? What could it *possibly* mean? And when you *knew* it, you had known *what?* And you said there is something else. A stag by the road, a pencil mark. Here is a story: she came to see me; a bowl, she brought a bowl of cherries, one fell on the book. She wrote: Here is the stain of an ice-cold cherry. Later when I had a book I filled in a spot. To be what? What does that mean? What Does That Mean to You? And when we die what will they say about us? What will they say? That he lived well in a terrible time. That I was such and such a man — and then *they* die. What could it mean? What could it possibly mean? Or if they said it about you and me. You saw a stag on the road.

CLAIRE.   *(Pause.)* Yes. *(Pause.)*

JOSEPH.   You came up with Michael. *(Pause.)*

CLAIRE.   Yes.

JOSEPH.   You said "The highway." I don't know. You say "send me a sign." He sends a sign. You say that it is inconclusive. *(Pause.)*
"Pigeons on the lawn
The flight of birds
A taste of copper in the mouth"
is that what you wanted to hear? *(Pause.)*

CLAIRE.   I'm sorry ... *(Pause.)*

JOSEPH.   "Here is the stain of an ice-cold cherry."

End

NO ONE
WILL BE IMMUNE

NO ONE
WILL BE IMMUNE

Two men. A and B.

A.   ... but when I saw the lights I thought I'd seen them
before and I thought, "Yes. That's just ...," then I couldn't
think it was just *what*, because what could it be?

B.   What could it have been?

A.   It could have been ... what could it have been? It could
have been a ... car. A car with a machine on top. A *police* car.
An ... *aid* car. Someone coming to aid. But it was not. It was
white light. *White* light, do you know. Pure white, I remember
thinking that it was not in the least yellow. Not in the least.
And I thought that it could have been an *opening*, of some
sort.

B.   An opening?

A.   Yes.

B.   To do what?

A.   To do what?

B.   Yes.

A.   To ... to do what? *(Pause.)* To do what...? A *supermarket*
opening. A ... what did...?

B.   ... yes.

A.   What did you mean?

B.   That's right.

A.   You meant ... you meant ... I said an Opening, I meant
Of a Store. Or something. But you meant An Opportunity.

B.   That's what I thought you meant.

A.   You thought that's what I meant.

B.   Yes.

A.   Or ... I see, An Opportunity to do what, though? Or ...
an opening, it could be, an opening *into* something. Which is,

yes, what we might mean if we say, and the word you used, was "opportunity." I often thought, if you could fill in the blanks. Of those things you misremembered, of those you forgot, as in a dream, or, do you see, a puzzle that you could not solve, the blanks, then you would have a story which, which, *another* story, do you see, which ...

B.   What are the blanks?

A.   The blanks? Are those things which you ...

B.   No. What are the blanks *here*?

A.   Here?

B.   Yes.

A.   In this. We have "Aid."

B.   "Aid."

A.   ... I could not remember.

B.   ... what the *cars* were to do.

A.   Yes.

B.   "Aid."

A.   And, "an opening." In *this* case, do you see, with lights. Scanning the sky. And why "a supermarket," rather than a *film*? Don't you think? *That's* mundane. "A Supermarket Opening."

B.   ... could it have been another sort of shop?

A.   What difference. "A Shop Opening." Its radius was too small.

B.   What was? The light?

A.   In the sweep it made. Yes.

B.   It was sweeping the heavens.

A.   "Sweeping the Heavens." How Sweet. Yes. But so it was. In this tight arc. In this tight arc of opening. Yes. Nothing escapes you. What a man you are. Sweeping the Heavens. A searchlight.

B.   It formed a cone.

A.   Did it?

B.   You said it did.

A.   Yes. It did.

B.   Are you amending that?

A.   I'm not amending it. No. "Then why did I hesitate?" It sees a violation. To me, and I say it's not your fault. Isn't that charming of me? But but, having it *reiterated*. In my words. You know? As if they were "set." It was ambiguous. To say the least. *Although* I chose the words. Yes. I said them.

B.   You think that they don't do it justice.

A.   Is that what I think? And I looked out the window. It was flashing. *Whipping* around. Slowly. It would form this arc. A circle. As it came close to my side, it would *whip* through it. And it formed a cone.

B.   A narrow cone.

A.   A narrow cone. All right.

B.   Well, was it?

A.   Yes. It was. All right. A narrow ... any cone is narrow.

B.   Is it?

A.   At the point. You see: if one says *narrow,* that is only to describe the projected *height* of the cone.

B.   ... is that so?

A.   ... it seems to me. If we say *narrow,* then that is to say it seemed it was intended to rise, that the light was meant to travel over *distances. (Pause.)* You see. It could have been a helicopter. Landed, and shooting its beacon. That is to say, hovering, and playing its searchlight down. But it was not a helicopter. It was not a car. It was not a ... a ... and I broke out my shotgun. I loaded it. I started for the door. I started for the door. And I said "no." "I do not want to know. *(Pause.)* No. No." And I said to myself, "if you don't *go,* you will never know. What you saw." And I said, "Yes. I will never know. All right." And I stayed inside. I took out the shells. I put the shotgun up.

B.   Did you look at the window?

A.   No.

B.   Why not?

A.   I knew what was there. I fell asleep.

B.   Did you think that was odd?

A.   To fall asleep. When I was so ...

B.   Yes.

A.   *Later (Pause.)* You see. I awoke. I half-woke. And the light was in the yard. The half-light.

B.   In the yard.

A.   Yes.

B.   In the half-light.

A.   In the half-light. Yes. I told you.

B.   And it woke you up.

A.   There was. It seemed to me. A flash. A flash. The same white, white light. Unnaturally white. As ... *(Pause.)* as ... almost ... almost.... *(Pause.)* I was frightened. Lord. I was so frightened.

B.   Were you asleep? *(Pause.)*

A.   I don't know. *(Pause.)* I don't know. I don't think so.

B.   It was just outside your house.

A.   Yes. *(Pause.)* Isn't that something? What can that have meant? What sort of man can that be, who is reduced to say, "Yes. They came for me..."? What sort of man must that be? *(Pause.)*

B.   What is a "half-light?"

A.   ... I ... *(Pause.)*

B.   You said "My God." And they reported that you said "my child."

A.   ... it was all foreseen.

B.   It all was? What was?

A.   That, as if that were the magical phrase. It had the *power,* but it bore the *curse.* It had the *price,* you see? The moment that I uttered it, *before* I said it: how could I not know? Why did I *choose* it? And I wracked my mind for something *other* than ... I said "my baby" ... and I could not find it. Now: what can you think that means?

B.   I don't know what it means.

A.   It must mean something.

B.   Must it?

A.   What can it mean?

B.   Tell me.

A.   Tell you? That I, well, I, that I did not *want* to be forced to, forced ... that it was *necessary*.... *(Pause.)* That it was *necessary. (Pause.)* That, that, that, that ...

B.   Would you tell me, if you would, the exact words you used?

A.   If I remember them.

112

B. Tell me the best you can. It's all right. *(Pause.)* It's all right.

A. ... but why do I find it so ...

B. ... you find it...?

A. Because I could not find an alternative phrase. Because my *mind* ... my mind was ... on the point of death. I had to *speak*. I had *to speak out.*

B. On the point of death. You said:

A. I've told you. But I'll tell you.

B. You said:

A. "Oh my God. My baby!"

B. And you told them...?

A. What did they report?

B. Please tell me what you told to them.

A. I told them ...

B. Yes.

A. ... that I had left my child.

B. You'd left it.

A. That, yes, that it was my ... *not* my child. You see? I wouldn't, I couldn't have *said* my child.

B. You said your child *now.*

A. Now. Yes.

B. Why?

A. Because I *heard* it. You're the one who said it.

B. I said it.

A. *I* said "my baby."

B. And if you *had* said "your child?"

A. I couldn't have said it.

B. But if you had.

A. I'd have had to've ... "corrected" it.

B. And how would you have done that?

A. I ...

B. As if this were then.

A. I'd have said ... I don't know.

B. Tell me.

A. That, that, I don't know, that this was my "day."

B. Your day.

A. I'd picked it up at *school,* I suppose.

B.   ... boy or girl...?

A.   ... and *taken* it ...

B.   ... to?

A.   I don't know. But, and why? I never told them.

B.   You did not?

A.   No.

B.   Tell me now. In your mind.

A.   In my mind.

B.   Where had you left her?

A.   In. It was. A ... a *playground*. A ... no, I've ... what difference can it make?

B.   I don't know. That's why I ...

A.   Something ... something.

B.   A girl?

A.   What?

B.   It was a girl you'd left?

A.   I don't know.

B.   What did you see when you said it?

A.   I said "baby."

B.   Yes. All right.

A.   I said "baby."

B.   Well. Say it now. What do you see?

A.   A child?

B.   Yes.

A.   How old?

B.   That's what I'm ...

A.   How old? Two.

B.   Two years.

A.   Yes.

B.   Is a two-year-old at school?

A.   Is it? I don't know. How would *I* know?

B.   Think, now. Think, now.

A.   I was speaking, I ...

B.   Think now, and tell me. Does ... at what age does a child go to school?

A.   At five.

B.   Not earlier?

A.   I think. Yes. To a nursery.

B.   At two?

A.   No.

B.   That's too young.

A.   Yes.

B.   Where should it be?

A.   With its mother.

B.   And why wasn't it then?

A.   It ... it was my "day."

B.   So, then, you would have taken it?

A.   Yes.

B.   From its mother.

A.   Yes.

B.   And took it where?

A.   ... to ...

B.   ... to a playground.

A.   To a playground? No.

B.   No.

A.   I know where I would have took it, but I don't want to say.

B.   Why?

A.   Because. Because. I don't like it because ...

B.   Yes?

A.   It's *tawdry*.

B.   Tawdry.

A.   It's banal. What *can* this be in aid of? For not only did I never *say* it, but I have just demonstrated why, for *had* I said it, when it could not be unsaid, I'd be responsible, for *gaps*, for *knowledge*, which I could not know, which is why I did *not* say it. My *plan* ...

B.   It was a good plan.

A.   It *was* a good plan. Yes. It *was* a good plan. "My baby." It was a *fine* plan.

B.   And what are the criteria?

A.   It *worked*.

B.   It worked.

A.   It got me off the plane. It saved my life.

B.   It was a good plan, and it saved your life.

A.   It forced them to turn back. You see? It forced them

back. My mind raced. I had seconds. *Seconds.* And I had to think. What would convince them? What would allow me. To speak. To force them ...

B.   Were you frightened?

A.   ... to ... of *course* I ... *I* don't know. Of *course* I was frightened. And the only thought was: I had *seconds.* After which ... *(Pause.)*

B.   And then that was a good plan?

A.   Should I have died?

B.   And so they turned back.

A.   They turned back.

B.   You said, "Oh. My God. I've left my Baby."

A.   That's right.

B.   And then they turned back.

A.   That's right.

B.   What did the pilot say?

A.   Ladies and Gentlemen, we have to return to the gate one moment, and ...

B.   Did he say he was experiencing Mechanical Difficulties?

A.   How could he? I was screaming. In the aisle.

B.   You were screaming?

A.   They all *knew* why we turned back.

B.   Why did you turn back?

A.   To let me off.

B.   To let you off.

A.   Yes.

B.   And so the plan worked?

A.   Yes.

B.   A good plan.

A.   Yes.

B.   As it let you live.

A.   I think it was.

B.   And what about the others. On the plane? *(Pause.)*

A.   What about them?

B.   What it a good plan for them?

A.   It wasn't a plan for them at all. *(Pause.)* It was a plan for me. Yes. All right. Yes. It was ... do you see? I wasn't *sure.* I was sure enough to "divert" the plane, but I wasn't ...

B.   To "divert" the plane.

A.   ... to ... to ...

B.   You "weren't sure"...?

A.   I couldn't stand the *ridicule*. How could I stand that? IF IT FLEW. You understand? IF IT FLEW.... No. If It Did *Not* Fly ...

B.   All right.

A.   No. If the plane had not flown. If I ... how were they to know? If I'd spoken up. If I had spoken up, but the plane did *not* fly. How were they ever to know? *Tell* me that? N'brand me as a lunatic. If I'd stopped the plane. If I told them: This Plane Must Must Not Land. And, and then, nothing happened. I would have been ... "This plane's going to explode".... "How do you know"...? *Beyond* a laughingstock, and ...

B.   ... how did you know?

A.   I told you.

B.   Yes. *(Pause.)*

A.   I saw the light.

B.   You saw the white light.

A.   Yes.

B.   And you knew what that meant.

A.   Yes.

B.   What did it mean?

A.   The Plane ...

B.   Yes. All right. Through what agency?

A.   A ... what would cause the explosion?

B.   Yes.

A.   I don't know.

B.   Mmm.

A.   A *bomb*. A ...

B.   Lightening?

A.   No.

B.   Collision?

A.   No.

B.   A Bomb?

A.   Yes. I told you. Possibly. I don't know.

B.   Did you want it to explode?

A.   Did I *want* it to? *No. No.*

B.   No?

A.   What possible. No. What *possible* motive could I have...? How can you *say* that? How can you *say* that?

B.   You said "What could I do. I could not tell them 'this plane must not land.'"

A.   I *couldn't* tell them that. They would have thought me ... *wait* a moment. *(Pause.)* Wait. *Wait* a moment. "This plane must not *fly*." *(Pause.)* *Wait* a moment. You're saying. That I could have said. What? Something, something. I could have said. Even *though* I was unsure. To protect the others.

B.   I don't know. Could you?

A.   What? To get them to ... "cancel" the plane. Yes? What?

B.   You got them to stop it long enough for *you* to get off.

A.   I, I could have said something to get them to stop it altogether.

B.   Perhaps?

A.   What? I could have, what? I could have said, "there's a *bomb* on the plane."

B.   How would you know that?

A.   I, I, if I'd *put* it there.

B.   Did you? *(Pause.)*

A.   Well. You see. You see. You see. This is the problem. This is the problem. *You brand yourself for life.* What is a man's responsibility? Had I, if I had said, "I've put a bomb on the plane." How can you ask me to do that? And the plane *stops*. They *search* the plane. They find *nothing*. *Nothing*. They find nothing. I am sent to prison. Prison. For the rest of my life. Because I spoke up.

B.   "You saw a light."

A.   ... for the rest of my life. What am I to say? The plane. Returns to the Gate. They search. "I lied. I misspoke myself. It's *not* a bomb on the plane. I lied. I misspoke myself. I had a *Premonition* ..."

B.   You didn't say that you "had a premonition."

A.   I said that I saw a light. When I saw it. I knew what it meant.

B.   What did it...?

A.   That the plane was going to crash. "And then you let those other people die..." I ... *(Pause.)*

B.   You had a premonition.

A.   I saw the light. Had I not been on the plane, had I called. Had I called a *friend,* and said, "I've had this vision."

B.   Then what?

A.   They would know.

B.   Who would know?

A.   Everyone.

B.   And they would know what?

A.   I was right.

B.   Yes. And the people on the plane?

A.   I could have called the airport.

B.   Yes.

A.   And said. Ah. If I said "I've had a vision," would they have stopped it then?

B.   I don't know.

A.   Mmm.

B.   What do you think you'd have had to say to stop it?

A.   I don't know.

B.   If you had seconds...?

A.   "There's a bomb on the plane."

B.   You saw the white light.

A.   Yes.

B.   You'd seen it before.

A.   I told you.

B.   Will you tell me again?

A.   In the field.

B.   Up in the Country?

A.   Yes.

B.   You thought that that light was...?

A.   ... something ... something ...

B.   ... that it had been a beacon.

A.   A beacon, something, yes.

B.   ... to objects in the sky.

A.   What could I think? What other use could it be? Shining?

B.   What comes to your mind. When you think of it?

A.   I don't know. I never saw that light before.

B.   Just the two times.

A.   Yes.

B.   Shining. What comes to your mind?

A.   A light.

B.   A light.

A.   A night light. I don't know. I don't know.

B.   A night light.

A.   ... I don't know.

B.   Who has a night light?

A.   I just meant. At night. A light in the night.

B.   You saw a night light.

A.   To, yes, to light the way.

B.   To light the way to where?

A.   In the dark.

B.   Yes. But to where?

A.   *I* don't know. How should *I* know?

B.   Who has a night light?

A.   I ... a *child*, certainly. A *child* uses it. Yes. I see it. I meant a *light*, do you see? In The Night. There was no child in it.

B.   You said "my baby."

A.   To get them to turn back.

B.   Yes. Why did you say that?

A.   Because it was so *precious*, you see? It was the most precious thing. That I could say. Do you see? At the moment. To ...

B.   You say in your fantasy, if you ...

A.   Why do you call it that?

B.   Call it?

A.   It isn't fantasy. It was ...

B.   "A plan." Beg your ...

A.   It was your question. It wasn't my plan, it was your question to me. Do you see? *(Pause.)*

B.   All right.

A.   It was never my fantasy.

B.   Yes.

A.   You ask me to imagine, and when I do, you ridicule me.

B.   Yes. I'm sorry. You, if you *had* left the child.

A. But it *wasn't* a child.

B. Yes. I know that.

A. It *wasn't* ...

B. Yes. Yes. Yes. It wasn't a child. It was a book.

A. No. It wasn't a book. It was a manuscript.

B. It was a manuscript.

A. Yes.

B. Of what?

A. Well. It wasn't real.

B. It was not.

A. No. I *told* you that.

B. It wasn't real.

A. No. It was ...

B. This was your 'plan'.

A. Yes. "I've left my baby.... Oh, my God. I've left my baby." that was all I said. There was no "child" in it. You've put that there.

B. I've asked you, if there *were* a child ...

A. But there *was* no child.

B. And there was no book?

A. Yes. There was a book. There *was* no book, but there was a manuscript. In my *plan*.

B. But it was not real.

A. The manuscript?

B. Yes.

A. It was in my *plan*. And then I told them. At the *gate*. This was my plan, you see, and why a child ... "you had misunderstood. There is no child. I said 'my *baby*' ... I have left My Baby ...

B. And your baby was?

A. A book. My book. It's my "child." Do you see? My *manuscript*. Years of work.

B. But there was no manuscript.

A. I've told you that.

B. It was part of a plan.

A. To ... yes. I would say "my baby," they would take me back. They'd say "how did you leave your baby?" And I'd say "I lay it down, and I forgot it." And they'd say, "Lay *it*

121

down...?" And I'd say something, something, and it would come out it was a *book*. No. No. A book could be replaced. A *manuscript*. I had been working on for *years*. And what could they do? If I'd said "a child," they could ... "check on it" ... couldn't they ...

B.   Why ... why ... you wouldn't have left a child ...

A.   No.

B.   Why not?

A.   Who would leave a child?

B.   Tell me.

A.   Even a sick man would, don't you think? I would think, keep track of it. If it was a child.

B.   If it were a child.

A.   If it were theirs.

B.   It would be a sick man to leave it.

A.   Yes.

B.   And who would leave a book he'd worked on. All those years?

A.   It was an accident.

B.   I understand. But if you *heard* that, what would you say?

A.   People do it all the time.

B.   They do?

A.   I've heard of cases of it.

B.   You have?

A.   People leaving things.

B.   Yes?

A.   Precious things.

B.   What?

A.   Violins, mostly. *(Pause.)*

B.   Is that it?

A.   Famous violins. Stradivarii. Yes. *You've* heard that. People, lost in a cab, maestros, rushing, rushing about, and they've left, as I said, they left their violin in a cab, every *year* you hear cases.

B.   And what do you think?

A.   What you hear it? "The dumb fool." *(Pause.)*

B.   What would the book have been about?

A.   I don't know.

B. Can ...

A. Just like an author. You see? With a manuscript. How should *I* know? 'Til it's done.

B. You saw it taking shape.

A. Well ... *vaguely* ...

B. Call it something now.

A. Yes?

B. Can you?

A. What I would say now?

B. Yes.

A. That it was about ...

B. That's right.

A. "The ..."

B. ... yes?

A. ... "Story Of My Life."

B. And you had left it. *(Pause.)*

A. It had been stolen.

B. Stolen.

A. Yes.

B. It's all the same. Isn't it? Lost or stolen; if you did not notice it. What would you say, of a man, who'd written, The Story of His Life, and allowed it ...

A. Wait. Wait. There *was* no book. It was a *story* ...

B. All right. In the Story. Let me ask you this. The book was stolen.

A. Yes.

B. Why would somebody steal it? As it had no value at all, but to you? Why would someone do that?

A. It was a senseless act.

B. But ...

A. Wait, no. I, if they *asked* me, you see, I say, "How would *I* know...?" *That's* all I have to say. *I* didn't steal it. Why should I arouse suspicions, by defending an act which is indefensible, no, the point is not that it's indefensible, but it's injurious to *me* ... *why* did he steal it...? I. Don't Know.

B. Describe it.

A. Manuscript so-by-so, green, red corners.

B. It have a title?

A. I'd been working on it. But it had no title.

B. Nothing on the cover?

A. I don't want to say that, you see: if they *look* for it, if they *look* for it, then it might not "tally" with the thing they find.

B. They can find nothing, for it's not real. *(Pause.)* They'll *never* find it. *(Pause.)* You may describe it all you want.

A. I didn't have a title. I don't like to *rush* to it, before I know ... you see? Before I really know ...

B. And *what* was it about?

A. The story of my life.

B. You said if there were one place you would leave a child, you said one word, and it was "bank" ...

A. Yes.

B. But where did you tell them that you'd left the book.

A. A hardware store.

B. A hardware store. What were you doing there?

A. I was not *in* the store.

B. I understand that. But *had* you been there ...

A. ... why should I have been there?

B. Wouldn't they want to know why you'd been in the store?

A. But what could be more innocent?

B. More innocent than any other store?

A. No. Certainly not.

B. Then, if they'd said: "Why had you been there?"

A. I ...

B. You can't say that you Wouldn't Want to Say ...

A. No. Of course not. I needed batteries.

B. If they said Where Were Those Batteries...?

A. Ah. Yes. They must be somewhere. Yes. I see.

B. You see?

A. I Put Them In My Flashlight.

B. If they said "where *is* this flashlight?"

A. I would say "in my home."

B. Do you have a flashlight in your home?

A. I ... I must have.

B. Do you?

A.   I don't know. I think so.

B.   You see? For it has to be there.

A.   Yes. I see. I *do* see that.

B.   Then do you have one?

A.   I *think* so.

B.   You think so.

A.   Yes.

B.   For if it's not there, then they'll say "where *is* it?"

A.   Yes. And it can't have "slipped" me, because I was just, I just bought the batteries.

B.   Put yourself in the home. Put yourself there.

A.   All right.

B.   The lights go out. *(Pause.)* If the *lights* go out ...

A.   Yes.

B.   What do you do?

A.   Ah. I have this light in the closet. Yes. It's a flashlight. It plugs in. If the *electricity* goes out, it comes on. Automatically.

B.   It does.

A.   Yes. And you can *remove* it, you see?

B.   Yes.

A.   And use it as a light.

B.   Yes.

A.   You see...?

B.   Yes.

A.   You see?

B.   Yes. A night light.

A.   I don't understand.

B.   The night light. It was in your closet.

A.   I told you that.

B.   Why was it in there?

A.   To *shield* me. Should it go *dark.*

B.   ... yes?

A.   To *shield* me. *(Pause.)* Should ... but, but, you see, I.... *(Pause.)*

B.   If it should go dark.

A.   Yes.

B.   You'd be frightened.

A.   Yes.

B.   But you said the *light* frightened you, too.

A.   What ... yes. The light.

B.   Because the light meant?

A.   The plane was going to explode.

B.   You said "crash."

A.   I did?

B.   Yes.

A.   When?

B.   Previously.

A.   What's the difference?

B.   Really.

A.   I *meant* crash. The light frightened me. Yes.

B.   Which light?

A.   Which?

B.   Yes.

A.   In the Country.

B.   In the Field.

A.   Yes.

B.   That light frightened you.

A.   That's right.

B.   I said A Light, and you told me that it meant the plane was going to crash.

A.   That's right.

B.   The light that night in the *field* ... it meant that?

A.   No.

B.   It meant *something* ...

A.   That's right.

B.   That you said you didn't want to know.

A.   No.

B.   Why not?

A.   I felt, I felt ...

B.   What did you feel?

A.   No, you see, you see, I'll tell you: I ... *(Pause.)* What I felt, was this: that I did not want to attract their attention.

B.   Yes...?

A.   Isn't that awful?

B.   Why?

A. It's unmanly.

B. It's...?

A. That I was *frightened* of them.

B. And what would they've done to you?

A. I don't know. How should I know?

B. Something.

A. Yes. Certainly.

B. Yes.

A. That's why. I didn't want their notice.

B. They would force you to *do* something.

A. Yes.

B. Should they come for you.

A. Yes. I said that.

B. And we don't know *what*.

A. What?

B. ... they would force you to do.

A. No.

B. But they came for you. They *did* come for you.

A. Did they?

B. After the light in the field. You saw.

A. I'm not sure.

B. You said you awoke. One moment. For a second. "And the light was in the yard."

A. I may have said that. But I'm not sure of that part.

B. But, you would say, that you *had* drawn their notice.

A. I don't know.

B. And felt that they were angry.

A. ... I ...

B. If you had not drawn their notice, why did they come down from the field?

A. I don't know.

B. It must have been for *you*, must it not?

A. I don't know.

B. Why else could it have been?

A. I don't know.

B. Why else? *(Pause.)*

A. I don't know. Yes. It must have been for me.

B. Mustn't it?

A.   Yes.

B.   To force you to do what?

A.   Who said it was to force me?

B.   You did.

A.   No. I didn't.

B.   You said that if they came for you, it would be to force you to do something, "against your will."

A.   What?

B.   I don't know.

A.   *I* don't know.

B.   No. What *sort* of thing?

A.   Something one would not do regularly.

B.   Yes. And why you?

A.   Why me?

B.   Yes.

A.   ... because, because ... I've *told* you ...

B.   ... yes?

A.   I'd *angered* them.

B.   How had you done so?

A.   By *spying*.

B.   Spying.

A.   Yes.

B.   You were spying on them?

A.   Yes.

B.   How?

A.   I saw them.

B.   Doing what?

A.   I don't know.

B.   You don't know. Why?

A.   Why? Because I was *sleepy*. I don't know. I couldn't *see* that far ...   I couldn't *see* it. It was a light.

B.   Just a light.

A.   Not just a light. This terrible ... this terrible ...

B.   They came to punish you.

A.   I don't know. I don't know. These are just feelings. Feelings. Do you know? I was so tired. I can't make them out. I can't make them out.

B.   You said that you have no child.

A.   No.

B.   ... you ...

A.   ... you know that.

B.   ... and that's why the book ...

A.   I said the book. Because I have no child.

B.   So you could claim to have something.

A.   Yes.

B.   Something.

A.   Yes.

B.   To call you home.

A.   To call me home. Yes.

B.   Some reason.

A.   Yes.

B.   So you said "A book."

A.   A, not a book, a manuscript.

B.   But there was not a manuscript?

A.   No. I invented it. Because I have no child. So I ... my "Work" ...

B.   Your "work" ...

A.   ... yes.

B.   But you *have* no ...

A.   In my *fantasy*. You see? My *fantasy*. To Call Me Home.

B.   To summon you.

A.   Yes.

B.   The light in the field. You said that you should not have looked.

A.   Did I say that?

B.   Isn't that why they wanted revenge?

A.   ... I don't know.

B.   Because you looked.

A.   I don't know.

B.   If you had not looked, would they have punished you?

A.   No.

B.   ... then...?

A.   I didn't *want* to look.

B.   ... I know that.

A.   ... I ...

B.   When you had seen it, then it was too late.

129

A.   Yes.

B.   When you knew what it was.

A.   It was, it was ... how could you *not* look?

B.   At the light in the field ... you said the light was calling.

A.   Yes.

B.   Calling.

A.   Summoning something.

B.   "Summoning."

A.   Yes.

B.   As you were summoned home. *(Pause.)* From the plane.

A.   The word's the same, yes.

B.   Those on the plane ...

A.   Yes...?

B.   People on the plane. Were they going?

A.   ... I ...

B.   Home. They were going home...?

A.   They, many places.

B.   Yet you said that they were going home.

A.   All right.

B.   You said that.

A.   Not *all* of them, I don't think.

B.   Those who were not...?

A.   Well, *work.*

B.   To work. Or to their home.

A.   Yes.

B.   To their wives.

A.   Yes.

B.   To children. To their *work* ...

A.   ... I don't know ...

B.   If they were anxious to get there ... wouldn't it seem...?

A.   I don't know.

B.   Why don't you?

A.   I made the plan in a *moment.* I saw they were anxious. *I* would be. *I* would be. To be traveling. If I were going home. Wouldn't you be? To something *important.* You see? To their *children.* To work. Here I was, to interrupt their plans. I didn't want. To *anger* them. If I said ... "There's a ..." So I said *that thing.* To stop it. That I knew. That thing they could

respect. That they could *understand.* I said "my baby."
B. And you didn't want to anger them.
A. No.
B. When you drew their notice.
A. Whom?
B. You said "a hardware store."
A. That's right.
B. You didn't want to say it.
A. No.
B. Why not?
A. I thought it stupid. I thought it banal. I thought: what a stupid place to tell them.
B. Yes?
A. That's right.
B. Yes? Then why did you think of it?
A. It just came to my mind.
B. Why?
A. *Why?* *I* don't know. I'd just *been* in one.
B. Yes? When?
A. Just the day before.
B. Yes? To buy what?
A. What? To buy the light. I told you.
B. To buy the light.
A. The light in the closet.
B. And why?
A. What?
B. Why did you buy the light?
A. What?
B. The light. *(Pause.)*
A. I was frightened. *(Pause.)*
B. Yes. You were frightened.
A. I *(Pause.)* I was frightened. To be alone.
B. You were?
A. Yes.
B. Since? *(Pause.)*
A. Since the Country?
B. Yes.
A. Since the ... since the *incident.* Up in the Country.

131

B.   Yes?

A.   I. You know. It made me feel a child.

B.   A child.

A.   To sleep. With the door. With the door half-open. And the light. I was "frightened": is that so terrible? If it happens to *you*, you see, then you'd know. I was *frightened*. By what I *saw*.

B.   What did you see?

A.   I don't *remember*.

B.   Where were you taking the plane to?

A.   Back to the country. You knew that.

B.   Why would you return there? If you were frightened?

A.   Why? To *show* them.

B.   ... to show them?

A.   To make an effort. You see? To *show* them. To *conquer* them, do you see? To strike back.

B.· You were angry.

A.   Was I? Yes.

B.   You said a beacon. *(Pause.)* You said it was a beacon. In the field.

A.   What?

B.   It was a beacon.

A.   Yes.

B.   *Summoning* someone.

A.   Summoning them. Yes. That was all that I could think. It was calling them. Calling someone. It was summoning them to earth.

NEW PLAYS

• **MERE MORTALS by David Ives, author of** *All in the Timing.* Another critically acclaimed evening of one-act comedies combining wit, satire, hilarity and intellect -- a winning combination. The entire evening of plays can be performed by 3 men and 3 women. ISBN: 0-8222-1632-9

• **BALLAD OF YACHIYO by Philip Kan Gotanda.** A provocative play about innocence, passion and betrayal, set against the backdrop of a Hawaiian sugar plantation in the early 1900s. *"Gotanda's writing is superb ... a great deal of fine craftsmanship on display here, and much to enjoy."* --Variety. *"...one of the country's most consistently intriguing playwrights..."* --San Francisco Examiner. *"As he has in past plays, Gotanda defies expectations..."* --Oakland Tribune. [3M, 4W] ISBN: 0-8222-1547-0

• **MINUTES FROM THE BLUE ROUTE by Tom Donaghy.** While packing up a house, a family converges for a weekend of flaring tempers and shattered illusions. *"With MINUTES FROM THE BLUE ROUTE [Donaghy] succeeds not only in telling a story -- a typically American one with wide appeal, about how parents and kids struggle to understand each other and mostly fail -- but in notating it inventively, through wittily elliptical, crisscrossed speeches, and in making it carry a fairly vast amount of serious weight with surprising ease."* --Village Voice. [2M, 2W] ISBN: 0-8222-1608-6

• **SCAPIN by Molière, adapted by Bill Irwin and Mark O'Donnell.** This adaptation of Molière's 325-year-old farce, *Les Fourberies de Scapin,* keeps the play in period while adding a late Twentieth Century spin to the language and action. *"This SCAPIN, [with a] felicitous adaptation by Mark O'Donnell, would probably have gone over big with the same audience who first saw Molière's Fourberies de Scapin...in Paris in 1671."* --N.Y. Times. *"Commedia dell'arte and vaudeville have at least two things in common: baggy pants and Bill Irwin. All make for a natural fit in the celebrated clown's entirely unconventional adaptation."* --Variety [9M, 3W, flexible] ISBN: 0-8222-1603-5

• **THE TURN OF THE SCREW adapted for the stage by Jeffrey Hatcher from the story by Henry James.** The American master's classic tale of possession is given its most interesting "turn" yet: one woman plays the mansion's terrified governess while a single male actor plays everyone else. *"In his thoughtful adaptation of Henry James' spooky tale, Jeffrey Hatcher does away with the supernatural flummery, exchanging the story's balanced ambiguities about the nature of reality for a portrait of psychological vampirism..."* --Boston Globe. [1M, 1W] ISBN: 0-8222-1554-3

• **NEVILLE'S ISLAND by Tim Firth.** A middle management orientation exercise turns into an hilarious disaster when the team gets "shipwrecked" on an uninhabited island. *"NEVILLE'S ISLAND ... is that rare event: a genuinely good new play..., it's a comedic, adult LORD OF THE FLIES..."* --The Guardian. *"... A non-stop, whitewater deluge of comedy both sophisticated and slapstick.... Firth takes a perfect premise and shoots it to the extreme, flipping his fish out of water, watching them flop around a bit, and then masterminding the inevitable feeding frenzy."* --New Mexican. [4M] ISBN: 0-8222-1581-0

DRAMATISTS PLAY SERVICE, INC.
440 Park Avenue South, New York, NY 10016 212-683-8960 Fax 212-213-1539
postmaster@dramatists.com www.dramatists.com

• TAF ... f the world's
greates ... t him under
the scr ... *e and deeply*
movin ... *een art and*
politic ... *nday Times.*
[4M, 3

• M ... t comedies,
MISSI ... 's foremost
drama ... *anley has an*
unusu ... *which people*
talk th ...], KISSING
CHRI

• TH ...
autho ...
Best B ...
length ...
Yorker ...
cultura ...
Times.

• MA ...
Play. ...
Terren ...
unforg ...
white- ...
theatr ...

• DE ... n addicted
to gan ... . "*... make*
tracks ... *azor-sharp*
dissect ... *-- a witty,*
wisecr ... *tinctive ...*
charac ... *Out (New*
York).

• RI ... debut of
one o ... *singly and*
effecti ... *urface of a*
numb ... *one of the*
vital ... *ay they say*
them.

440 Park Avenue South, New York, NY 10016 212-683-8960 Fax 212-213-1539
postmaster@dramatists.com www.dramatists.com